Understanding the Government of God

By

James L. Monteria

CLM Publications & Publishing, LLC
P.O. Box 932 Chesterfield, VA 23832

All rights reserved. No part of this book may be reproduced without written permission from the publisher, except for use of brief review for the furthering of the Kingdom of God. Unless otherwise indicated; all Scriptures are taken from the King James Version of the Bible

CLM Publications & Publishing, LLC
P.O. Box 932
Chesterfield, VA 23832

www.clmpublication.info

ISBN: 978-0-9897704-6-0

Cover Design/Graphics: Shelly E. Middleton
Author: James L. Monteria
Associate Editor: January Scott and Carrie Gay

Copyright © 2016 by CLM Publications & Publishing, LLC Printed in the United States of America; All rights reserved under International Copyright Law. Contents and cover may not be reproduce in whole or in part in any form without the expressed written consent of the publisher.

Table of Contents
"Understanding the Government of God"

1) Introduction — Page 1
2) Understanding the Kingdom of God Government — Page 9
3) Keys To The Kingdom of Heaven — Page 24
4) The Kingdom of God Power source is the Holy Spirit — Page 32
5) Kingdom System of Communication — Page 57
6) The Kingdom of God Ambassador — Page 70
7) What is the Church? How is the church Connect to the Kingdom of God? — Page 79
8) The Kingdom Law of Authority — Page 94
9) The Kingdom of God citizens dress code requirements while on earth — Page 105
10) The Kingdom of God operation of Faith — Page 120
11) Kingdom of God steps to Spiritual Maturity — Page 126
12) Manifestation of the Kingdom of God Sons/Daughters — Page 135
13) How to know if you are Operating in the Kingdom of God — Page 148
14) How to Enter the Kingdom of God — Page 160

Heavenly Decision — Page 174

Endnotes — Page 177

About the Author — Page 178

Acknowledgement

First, and foremost, I would not even know God, or be able to write anything about Him, were it not for His grace and mercy! I have come to appreciate the grace of God, the Lordship of Jesus Christ, and the Holy Spirit's presence in my life and my ministry, even more than words could express.

GUIDELINES FOR STUDY

A. Guidelines for Individual Study

1. Set aside a regular time each week when you can get alone with God and study the lessons in this manual.

2. Pray and ask the Lord to illuminate His Word to you as you study.

3. Look up each scripture and take time to think about (meditate on) the Word of God.

4. Move through the book at a steady pace and allow the Holy Spirit to minister to you personally.

B. Guidelines for Group Study

1. In group study, it is important to have one leader, preferably a mature Christian, who can facilitate the study each week.

2. Determine a regular time and a quiet location for weekly group meetings to study the lessons in this manual.

3. Pray and ask the Lord to illuminate His Word each week.

4. Look up the scriptures and take turns reading them aloud.

5. Encourage each person to participate. Do not allow one person to dominate the discussion.

6. Allow for group discussion and interaction during the lessons, but avoid distractions with unnecessary side issues.

7. Don't be in a hurry to complete the study; rather, maintain a steady pace through the lesson while allowing the Holy Spirit the freedom to minister to each individual in the group.

8. Assign the next lesson as homework each week. After the group members have completed their individual study, they will be more familiar with the material. Encourage group members to write down any questions they have and present them for discussion the next time you meet together.

The Kingdom of God and His Church!

Isaiah 9:6-7;

> "⁶For unto us a child is born, unto us a son is given: and **the government** shall be upon his shoulder: and his name shall be called Wonderful, Counsellor, The mighty God, The everlasting Father, The Prince of Peace. ⁷Of the **increase of his government** and peace there shall be no end, upon the throne of David, and upon his kingdom, to order it, and to establish it with judgment and with justice from henceforth even forever. The zeal of the Lord of hosts will perform this."

Matthew 16:15-18;

> Jesus said… "He saith unto them, But whom say ye that I am? ¹⁶And Simon Peter answered and said, Thou art the Christ, the Son of the living God. ¹⁷And Jesus answered and said unto him, Blessed art thou, Simon Barjona: for flesh and blood hath not revealed it unto thee, but my Father, which is in heaven. ¹⁸And I say also unto thee, that thou art Peter, and upon this rock I will build **my church**; and the gates of hell shall not prevail against it."

Chapter 1
Introduction

There must be a paradigm shift in the way Christians think. In order for the Church to be able to go where God has planned it to go and for us to do what God has planned for us to do in these last days, we must understand who we are, what we have been blessed with, and what is going on where we are.

God's plan is to rule (influence) earth with heaven's governmental system. The question is how was God going to accomplish this? God's plan was and still is to do it through his children (born-again believers), the children of man—mankind, and it was never God's intent for man to rule Heaven.

When God created Adam and fashioned Eve, He gave them authority over all the earth. Adam became the ruler over the earth or the god of this world. The fall of Adam (mankind) was a fall from rulership dominion in the earth and not a fall from Heaven.

You could almost say that Satan pulled off a coup when Adam literally disobeyed God, and caused him to turn the governing authority over planet earth into the hands of satan.

Now remember that Satan has been kicked out of the third Heaven and became the prince of the kingdom of darkness.

The word prince means ruler. He comes in and his goal was to take over the territory that Adam was to rule and protect. We must understand what happened. The present government authority that Adam had (which means he was ruling the earth for God) was now taken over and Adam became subject to another authority who was satan, the evil one, an enemy to the things of God. He dominated Adam.

The proper way to describe what had happened is what we call treason. Treason is only possible if you have been given authority. So for example, I leave you in charge of a store that I own and go away for a couple of years. You take the store and give it to someone else without my permission.

This is similar to what Adam did. God gave him authority and dominion over the earth. Adam then gave it to someone else through disobedience thus committing high treason. What is the penalty for treason? The penalty is death in every country, and it was true in this case because Adam and Eve died spiritually the moment they ate from the tree of knowledge of good and evil.

In *Genesis 3:15*, we have the first prophecy of how God would rescue and restore mankind (born-again believers) back to rulership in the earth. This prophecy was fulfilled in *Matthew 28:1-10* and *Colossians 2:15*.

Let us take a look at the process of how God went about rescuing mankind and reestablishing His Kingdom back on earth. This will help us to better understand the message of Jesus Christ and the Bible.

> *Isaiah 9:6-7* **says,** "6For unto us a child is born, unto us a son is given: and the government shall be upon his shoulder: and his name shall be called Wonderful, Counselor, the Mighty God, The Everlasting Father, the Prince of Peace.

> ⁷Of the increase of his government and peace there shall be no end, upon the throne of David, and upon his kingdom, to order it, and to establish it with judgment and with justice from henceforth even forever. The zeal of the Lord of hosts will perform this."

Many Christians say it is hard to be a Christian. I believe the reason for this is that we are operating or trying to live off the wrong platform. Many churches are still trying to use the old model of the church, "being religious," because that is what they do; however, that is not what is needed.

The prophecy of Jesus coming to earth from *Isaiah 9:6-7* states that some 700 years prior to Jesus being born in the earth, which took place some 2,000 years ago.

The reason that Jesus came to earth as a man was to redeem humankind back to God and to give us that which was lost. He reestablished the government of God back on earth. He paid the ransom that was needed because of the LOVE he has for us. Jesus came to bring mankind back to where they were before Adam sinned.

Think about this. When you ask average Christians about their relationship with God, they will say "I go to church" and will begin to speak about their religious practices.

Many Christians have not known of nor understood the government of God. The reason for this is that it has not been taught.

The prophecy was fulfilled the day that Jesus went into the synagogue to read on the Sabbath day.

> *Luke 4:16-20, Jesus said... "16 And he came to Nazareth, where he had been brought up: and, as his custom was, he went into the synagogue on the Sabbath day, and stood up for to read. 17 And there was delivered unto him the book of the prophet Esaias. And when he had opened the book, he found the place where it was written, 18 The Spirit of the Lord is upon me, because he hath anointed me to preach the gospel to the poor; he hath sent me to heal the brokenhearted, to preach deliverance to the captives, and recovering of sight to the blind, to set at liberty them that are bruised, 19 To preach the acceptable year of the Lord. 20 And he closed the book, and he gave it again to the minister, and sat down. And the eyes of all them that were in the synagogue were fastened on him."*
>
> *Matthew 4:17, Jesus said... "17 From that time Jesus began to preach, and to say, Repent: for the kingdom of heaven is at hand."*

Jesus preached and taught the Kingdom of God for his entire earthly ministry according to the four gospels and the first chapter of the book of Acts.

Jesus taught His disciples to pray, "Thy Kingdom come." This is because the church is being preached and not the Kingdom of God.

> *Matthew 6:9-13*, Jesus said... "⁹after this manner therefore pray ye: Our Father which art in heaven, Hallowed be thy name. ¹⁰ Thy kingdom come, Thy will be done in earth, as it is in heaven. ¹¹Give us this day our daily bread. ¹²And forgive us our debts, as we forgive our debtors. ¹³And lead us not into temptation, but deliver us from evil. For thine is the kingdom, and the power, and the glory, forever. Amen.

Why is it so important that we understand the Kingdom of God and the message of the kingdom? Because every person that is born into the earth is born into the kingdom of darkness!

> *Psalm 51:5*, David said, "Behold, I was shapen in iniquity; and in sin did my mother conceive me."

The only way to get **out** of the kingdom of darkness is to be BORN AGAIN.

> ***Romans 10:9-10,*** *"⁹That if thou shalt confess with thy mouth the Lord Jesus, and shalt believe in thine heart that God hath raised him from the dead, thou shalt be saved. ¹⁰For with the heart man believeth unto righteousness; and with the mouth, confession is made unto salvation."*

Jesus said to Nicodemus, "Except you be born again (born from above), you cannot see the Kingdom of God" (**see *John 3:1-5*)**.

Whether we understand it or, not every person that is born in the earth is born into the kingdom of darkness with the exception of Jesus.

When you are born again you are born into the Kingdom of God, Paul declares!

> ***Colossians 1:13,*** *"¹³Who hath delivered us from the power of darkness (kingdom of darkness), and hath translated us into the kingdom of his dear Son."* (Emphasis added).

The above verses show the exact reason why the church or the purpose for preaching the Gospel of the Kingdom of God. As mankind, we can then realize that we are in the kingdom of darkness and must be **born** into the Kingdom of God.

Summary

Prophesy of the Coming Kingdom (the Government of God), it is very important that we understand the Government of God. Let us look at another important scripture pertaining to the Kingdom (government) of God.

In *Matthew 16:15-18*, Jesus is prophesying about the Church. The reality and the role of the church is of such significance that I believe the majority of Christians have no understanding of it. It is imperative that we understand the church's significance. Jesus is not talking about something religious, but a legislative body of the government of God (**See *Revelation 11:15***).

Chapter 2
Understanding the Kingdom of God Government

Jesus preached and taught the Kingdom of God for his entire earthly ministry according to the four gospels and the first chapter of the book of Acts. Jesus taught His disciples to pray, "Thy Kingdom come." This is because the churches religion is being preached and not the Kingdom of God.

The prophets anticipated the coming of the Kingdom of God. In examining *Daniel 2:31-44*, the key verse is 35b. Daniel said in the interpretation of King Nebuchadnezzar's dream, "35Then was the iron, the clay, the brass, the silver, and the gold, broken to pieces together, and became like the chaff of the summer threshing floors; and the wind carried them away, that no place was found for them: and the stone that smote the image became a great mountain, and filled the whole earth." Most people have no idea when this happened.

The vision in the book of Daniel explains the prophecies from the time of Daniel to the time of Jesus Christ's second coming. Daniel understood that there would be four major world ruling empires during that time.

He explained that in the days of the fourth empire God will replace these human kingdoms with the Kingdom of God.

> *Daniel 2:44,* "*And in the days of these kings shall the God of heaven set up a kingdom, which shall never be destroyed: and the kingdom shall not be left to other people, but it shall break in pieces and consume all these kingdoms, and it shall stand forever.*"

> *Daniel 12:1-3,* "*And at that time shall Michael stand up, the great prince which standeth for the children of thy people: and there shall be a time of trouble, such as never was since there was a nation even to that same time; and at that time thy people shall be delivered, every one that shall be found written in the book. ²And many of them that sleep in the dust of the earth shall awake, some to everlasting life, and some to shame and everlasting contempt. ³And they that be wise shall shine as the brightness of the firmament; and they that turn many to righteousness as the stars forever and ever.*"

Understanding of the Kingdom of God and its divine government, When you really think about a kingdom it is synonymous to a government, but in this book,

we are talking about the Kingdom of God and His divine government. I have come to recognize that there are several groups of people in the world today.

There are the heathens (sinners), the religious (who have their way of getting to God), and the citizens of the Kingdom of God. Now for those who are serious about their citizenship in the Kingdom of God, I say this--study is for the serious citizens of the Kingdom of God.

- **What is the Kingdom of Heaven?** It is the spiritual home of God or the presence of God's third heaven.

    Isaiah 66:1 and Acts 7:49, "Heaven is my throne, and earth is my footstool"; and Revelation 4.

- **What is the Kingdom of God?** It is the invisible divine government in the spirit realm that is established on the earth when the will of its King has been carried out. (Archangels, Cherubims, Seraphims, and Angels **See** *Isaiah 9:6, 7.*)

- **What is the kingdom of darkness?** It is the invisible evil government in the spirit realm that is established on the earth by satan, who is the head, and when his will is being carried out in the earth. The devil's headquarters is the second heaven. Those who was inspire by Satan the unseen ruler illustrate the kingdom of darkness.

satan, who is in rebellion against God (*Matthew 12:24-30*) and is inferior to God's Kingdom. Jesus demonstrated this by casting demons out.

In examining the Holy Scriptures, *Ephesians 1:21, 3:10* and *Colossians 2:10; 15,* we see very clearly Jesus operating as a man who defeated satan, principalities, powers of the air, rulers of the darkness of this world, and spiritual wickedness in Heavenlies."

We find in the books of Acts that Philip and Paul preached and taught the Kingdom of God:

- *Acts 8:11-13*   Philip preached the Kingdom of God.
- *Acts 19:7-9*   Paul preached the Kingdom of God.
- *Acts 28:30-31* Paul preached the Kingdom of God.

Colossians 1:13, there is only one-way to enter the Kingdom of God and to be able to experience the kingdom life. That is to be born into it. When the Bible says we must be born again, in the original Greek it says we must be born from above. We are actually born from heaven, another government, another country, the Kingdom of God.

1. **What is a Kingdom?** It is the invisible divine government in the spirit realm that is established on the earth when the will of its King has been carried out by Archangels, Cherubims, Seraphims, and Angels. *(See Isaiah 9:6)*

The Kingdom of God also possesses these components. Here are some you will need to know in order to understand the concepts of scriptures. All kingdoms have:

- **A King and Lord – A Sovereign** - The king is the embodiment of the kingdom representing its glory and nature. Authority flows from the king and the word of the king is supreme.

- **A Territory – A Domain** - The territory is the domain over which the king exercises total authority. The territory, its resources, and its people are all personal property of the king. The king by right owns all and, therefore, is considered lord over all. The word lord denotes ownership by right. Lord is only given to one who is a sovereign owner. This is why the scriptures declare, "The earth is the Lord's and the fullness thereof; the world, and they that dwell therein" *(See Psalms 24:1)*.

- **A Constitution** – a Royal Covenant - The constitution is the covenant of the king with his citizenry, expresses the mind, and will for his citizens and the kingdom. The constitution is the documented words of the king. The Bible contains the constitution of the Kingdom of God which details His will and mind for His citizens.

- **A Citizenry – A Community of Subject** - The citizenry are the people that live under the rule of the king. Citizenship in a kingdom is not a right, but a privilege and is a result of the king's choice.

The benefits and privileges of a kingdom are only accessible to citizens and, therefore, the favor of the king is always a privilege. Once one becomes a citizen of the kingdom, all the rights of the citizenship are at the citizen's pleasure.

The king is obligated to care for and protect all of his citizens, and their welfare is a reflection on the king himself.

The number one goal of a citizen in a kingdom is to submit to the king seeking only to remain in right standing with him. This is called righteousness.

This is why Jesus said the priority of all men is to seek His kingdom *(Matthew 6:33)*.

- **Law – Acceptable Principles -** The law constitutes the standards and principles established by the king himself by which his kingdom will function and be administered.

The laws of a kingdom are to be obeyed by all including foreigners residing in it.

The laws of a kingdom are the ways by which one is guaranteed access to the benefits of the kingdom. Violations of the kingdom law places one at odds with the king and thus interrupts the favorable position one enjoys with the king. The laws in a kingdom cannot be changed by the citizens nor are they subject to citizen referendum or debate. Simply put, the word of the king is law in his kingdom. Rebellion against the law is rebellion against the king. King David understood this principle of royal word. *(See Psalm 138:3)*

- **Privileges – Rights and Benefits -** The privileges are the benefits the king lavishes on his faithful citizens. This aspect of the kingdom is very different from other forms of government. In a kingdom, citizenship is always desired by the people because once you are in the kingdom the king is personally responsible for you and your needs.

Also, because the king owns everything within his kingdom, he can give to any citizen any or all of his wealth as he desires.

- **A Code of Ethics** – Acceptable Lifestyle and Conduct - A code of ethics is the acceptable conduct of the citizens in the kingdom and their representation of the kingdom. The code includes moral standards, social relationships, personal conduct, attitude, attire, and manner of life.

- **An Army – Security** - The army is the kingdom's system of securing its territory and protecting its citizens. It is important to understand that in a kingdom the citizens do not fight in the army but enjoy the protection of the army.

This is why in the Kingdom of God the angels are called the "hosts of heaven." This word host means army and identifies the angels as the so-called military component of the kingdom of heaven. The kingdom concept presents a challenge to our religious thinking of the church as an army.

A careful study of the biblical constitution of the word will show that the church, as Jesus established it, is not identified as an army but rather a citizenship, a family of sons and a nation. *(See Psalm 78:49-50, 103:20-21, Matthew 13:40b-42).*

- **A Commonwealth** – Economic Security, a commonwealth is the economic system of a kingdom which guarantees each citizen equal access to financial security. In a kingdom, the term commonwealth is used because the king's desire is that all his citizens share and benefit from the wealth of the kingdom. The kingdom's glory is in the happiness and health of its citizens. Consider carefully the word of the king of the Kingdom of God, Jesus Christ. *(See Luke 12:22-24; Luke 12:31-32)*

- **A Social Culture** – Protocol and Procedures - The social culture is the environment created by the life and manners of the king and his citizens. This is the cultural aspect that separates and distinguishes the kingdom from all others around it.

It is the culture that expresses the nature of the king through the lifestyle of his citizens. This distinction in kingdom culture is evidenced in the words of the Lord Jesus, what He repeatedly said in the book of *Matthews 5:21-22, 20:26*. Kingdom social culture is supposed to be evident in our daily activities and encounters.

1. The Components of the Kingdom of Heaven

All kingdoms are comprised of a number of components necessary for them to function effectively. All kingdoms, including the Kingdom of God, are comprised of the following:

- **System of Administration** - God's original plan is to establish a kingdom of kings and extend His rulership, will, and nature from heaven to earth through the administrative leadership of mankind.

  The vehicle that will enable God to do this is by the person of the Holy Spirit.

- **Holy Spirit** - The person of the Holy Spirit was seen by Jesus immediately following His baptism *(Matthew 3:16)*. Just as the Father and the Son can be seen, so can the Holy Spirit. His descent as a dove does not mean that He flies around heaven like a dove. Nor does Jesus walk around heaven with the body of a lamb.

  > *Revelation 4:5, "5 And out of the throne proceeded lightnings and thunderings and voices: and there were seven lamps of fire burning before the throne, which are the seven Spirits of God.*

  The Holy Spirit was seen again as "seven lamps" of blazing fire. If the Holy Spirit came as a dove in Matthew, are we expecting Him to have a body made out of seven candles or seven pieces of fire?

  The Holy Spirit longs for a daily, ongoing personal relationship with you. It wants to make a mighty entrance into your life.

As we talk about the system administration, look at the example of the Holy Spirit in the lives of individuals in the Bible, *Acts 8:26;* Angel, in verse 29; the Holy Spirit spoke with *Philip 39; Acts 10:1-19; Acts 16:9; Romans 8:13-16.*

- **Health Program** – Healings *(See Isaiah 53:5, 1 Peter2:24)*
- **Education Program** – Teaching ministry of the Holy Spirit *(See John 16:13, 14:26)*
- **Taxation Systems** – Tithing *(See Malachi 3:8-10)*
- **Central Communication System** - Gifts of the Holy Spirit *(See 1 Corinthians 12:4-11)*
- **Diplomatic Corps** - Ambassadors of Christ skilled in dealing with sensitive matters or people and are able to take a broad view of negotiations between two kingdoms. *(See 2 Corinthians 5:17-21)*
- **An Economy** – A system of giving and receiving (seedtime and harvest time) *Genesis 8:20-22; Genesis 1:11, 12; Genesis 8:20-22; Galatians 6:7.* Before we touch on the Law of Seedtime and Harvest, I want to put first things first.

Priority wise tithing comes first and then you sow your seed *(Malachi 3:7-12)*.

Many Christians are missing it if they are trying to live off the seed. We are to know that our paycheck is the seed. We pay our tithes and then we sow our seed. As the harvest comes this is what we are to live off seed, and will meet any need. *(See 2 Corinthians 9:6-10)*

Scriptural example of a seed being required before a need was met in *Genesis 26:12,* "Then Isaac sowed in that land and received in the same year a hundredfold; and the LORD blessed him." Moses's commission to deliver the Israelites for Egyptian captivity included:

- Exodus 5– 2:1-13   Seed = a lamb = deliverance
- 1 Kings 17:8 – 16   Seed = a little calf = life
- Luke 7:36 – 48   Seed = alabaster box very precious ointment = salvation
- Luke 7:1-10   Seed = synagogue = healing of his servant
- Mark 2:1-5   Seed = roof = a friend being healed

Do you have to pay for your blessing? The answer is no. A careful study and the presentation of the message of the Kingdom of Heaven by Jesus will illustrate the presence of all these components and characteristics of life in the Kingdom of God.

Summary

The most outstanding element distinguishing the Kingdom of God from every other kingdom is the concept that all of its citizens are relatives of the king and are kings themselves. This was the message brought to the earth by the Lord Jesus Christ.

Chapter 3
Keys to the Kingdom of Heaven

To give a more comprehensive understand of the government of God; let us examine the concept of "keys" to operating in the Kingdom of Heaven. It is my hope that you now have a better understanding of how to use specific keys (laws and principles by which heaven operates). To open the doors that lead to greater understanding of the Government of the Kingdom of God, and the freedom and that you will ultimately experience all that God has for you as you apply His Word in every area of your life.

Success in the kingdom of God is learning the keys (laws and principles by which Heaven operates).

When Jesus said that He has given us the keys to the Kingdom of Heaven He was not talking about physical keys, but about the principles and laws by which heaven operates. *(See Matthew 18:13-19).*

The objective is to provide insight and understanding of these principles and laws so that you can apply your faith properly and experience success God's way.

Once you take hold of these laws and principles, believing them to the point of practical application, you can face with confidence any situation with which you are confronted.

You must also learn how to apply the right key to the right situation. Just as a vehicle operates using only the key that is specifically designed for it, the same is true with the Kingdom of Heaven. When applying your faith to God's Word, enacting the law and principles of the Kingdom of God, you ready to walk in Godly prosperity in every area of your life. As you apply these keys, law and principles (scriptures) with faith release through prayer, you will only enjoy success that God can bring into your life.

Keys are set up by God to produce a specific result that cannot be changed or altered. Your opinion, misguided prayer or your desire for a different outcome will not influence the result of a principle or law that has been set in motion by the Almighty God.

If you have what you feel is an unanswered prayer, examine the Word of God to see if you are trying to open some doors in heaven with the wrong key.

Once you find the right key that applies to your situation and act upon it in faith, you will see God move in answer to your prayer and your situation will change.

To help you further understand that the result of enacting a law or principle is fixed, God gave us natural laws as well as spiritual laws. For example, there is the Law of Gravity. It is design to pull everything to the center of the earth.

Gravity is a law, it is a principle, and it is a key. This is how God set it up and man can do nothing to change it. You cannot defy gravity.

Another example, if you climb to the top of a ten story building and jump off, gravity will have its way, pulling you down to the ground with the end result being your probable death. Another natural law is the Law of Lift. It is design to supersede the law of gravity when the correct parameters are in place. A bird in flight is a perfect example. Birds were design by God to naturally operate in the law of lift as their method of travel; we call this flying. Airplane travel is also an example of the law of lift in motion.

The supernatural law are activate through Faith. Though natural comprehension of this law eludes us as humans, we know that if we operate in it by faith, it will produce for us. Spiritual laws may not be understood, but as we trust in God, He cause them to work. He enjoy during things for his citizens. The key to success in life in the kingdom is learning the keys, laws and principles. We may not fully understand how these laws and principles work, but our objective is to obey them.

There are six main points to focus on when implementing the keys that God has given us.

Access (through faith) – the ability, right, or permission to approach, enter, speak with, or use; admittance. We have access to God Himself and all He owns when we operate in the Kingdom of Heaven *(Romans 9:4 NLT)*. For example, if I give you the key to my car, you now have access to my car and everything that is in it. It has been made available to you through the use of the key.

Authority – a power or right delegated or given As His children, God has delegated His power to us *(Luke 10:19 NKJV)* and given us the right through Him to call forth from the spirit realm into the natural realm whatever we need *(Romans 4:17)*. We must operate in the Kingdom Of Heaven to exercise our authority. Using the same example, when someone gives you the keys to their car, they have given you authority or the legal right to drive their car.

Ownership – legal right of possession we, as God's children, are joint heirs with Christ *(See Romans 8:17)*.

In the spirit realm, we already own all that God desires to bless us with but we must operate according to His kingdom principles if we are to experience the natural manifestation of that ownership.

For example, when you purchase a home or car and all the requirements are met, and all the papers have been signed, ownership transfers to you.

Knowledge and understanding applied Your knowledge and understanding of the laws and principles of the Kingdom of Heaven must be applied in order to produce the desired benefit. Without application, the benefits are available but never actually realized or experienced.

The Bible tells us that faith without works is dead. *(See James 2:20).*

Power – (Authority) to permit or to prevent As His children, we can walk in our God-given power through prayer *(James 5:16; Matt 18:19)*. When we pray according to His Word in faith, it releases God to move on our situation.

Through the power of prayer, we can thwart or even stop the attacks of the enemy against any other area of our lives. God gave us His power over all the power of Satan, our enemy *(**Luke 9:1 Contemporary English Version**).*

Freedom – the right to enjoy all the privileges or special rights of citizenship, membership, etc. *(Gal 5:1 NIV)* When we become citizens of heaven, we are able to experience the peace and security of being in Christ *(John 14:27)*. We are able to cast our cares upon the Lord, being released from the pressure and stress of worldly matters. To experience this God given peace, we must operate in the freedom of the Kingdom of Heaven.

What is the purpose of a principle?

1) Principles help to simplify life for you.
2) Principles help to protect and preserve your life.
3) Principles help to assist you in making decisions.

Summary

If you learn the principles of the kingdom, you will not have to pray for answers from God that He has already given as principles - principles are design to guide you in your decisions. Sometimes in our natural minds, we have a long list of do's and don'ts we think necessary to see God move after the expected period of interminable waiting.

We tend to make life harder than He intended. His principles are design to make life decisions a little easier for us.

Though Jesus had difficult periods in His life, His following the Father's principles helped Him to make simple decisions and to be at peace with them. He knew how to operate the keys, principles, precepts, and laws designed by His Father. **(See Matthew 8:5-12)**

Chapter 4
The Kingdom of God Power Source is the Holy Spirit

Introduction

We want to share with you knowledge of the Holy Spirit and the Power Source of the Kingdom of God. The reason that we need the Baptism of the Holy Spirit is because of several key things that He does as the third member of the Godhead. Within the Holy Scriptures, I will list several functions of the person of the Holy Spirit.

1. Who is the Holy Spirit?

The Holy Spirit is the third person of the Godhead or Trinity. The Trinity is made up of the Father, the Son, and the Holy Spirit.

Some examples of the manifestation of the Power Source of the Kingdom of God:

A. The Holy Spirit is a person, not an "it" or an impersonal Power Source of the Kingdom of God. We see the initial manifestation of the Holy Spirit in Genesis 1 and 2.

B. The Holy Spirit was came upon Jesus during His water baptism.

The Holy Spirit was the one who enabled Jesus to live and do the things that He did pertaining to the Kingdom of God--healing the sick, raising the dead, casting out demons, and all the other miraculous things that He did. *(See Matthew 3)*

C. On the day of Pentecost, the 120 disciples of Jesus in the Upper Room and the Holy Spirit was poured out upon them. *(See Acts 1-2)*

D. The book of Acts is really the Acts of the Holy Spirit through the Apostles. The Holy Spirit has gifts that are manifested in the life of the believer as He will.

These gifts will enable us to do exploits for God here on earth. Again, it is as The Holy Spirit wills. *(See 1 Corinthians 12:4-8)*.

They are not walking in the "supernatural" what God expects of us. Until we know this as a living reality, we will never be able to have a firm foundation that will cause us to be victorious Christians.

> ***1 John 4:4, says...*** *"⁴Ye are of God, little children, and have overcome them: because greater is he that is in you, than he that is in the world."*

When we realize that He is in us, we will begin to rely on the Greater One. When we begin to say to Him, "Greater One, I need a little assistance right now. I cannot do it myself. I need a little power." He will put it in overdrive, press down on the passing gear, and we will have the power we need to overcome every obstacle and every temptation.

We can talk to God. He is a divine person, and He has gifts that are available to be manifest in our lives as His will.

Until we know the living reality of the Indwelling Spirit, we can never have a firm foundation that will cause us to be victorious Christians. The ones who know the reality of the Indwelling Spirit, and walk in the light of it, will have a firm foundation causing them to be victorious Christians.

Every Christian is born of the spirit, but not every Christian is filled with the Holy Spirit. To be filled with the Holy Spirit does not save us. However, it does empower us to be able to live the Christian life (*doctrine of baptisms*, see *Hebrew 6:2*).

When I say we must know the reality of the Indwelling Spirit, I am talking to those who have been filled with the Holy Spirit, have had the experience of receiving the gift of the Holy Spirit, but are not walking in the fullness of the power.

2. What does it mean to be filled with the Holy Spirit

> ***Luke 4:1;*** *"And Jesus being full of the Holy Ghost returned from Jordan, and was led by the Spirit into the wilderness,"*
>
> ***Ephesians 5:18;*** *"Be filled with the Spirit,"*
> ***Romans 8:14*** *"For as many as are led by the Spirit of God, they are the sons of God,"*

The Baptism of the Holy Spirit

There are three baptisms spoken of in the Bible. This chapter will enlighten you on the baptism of the Holy Spirit and the importance of them.

The scriptures of the Bible that come from the book of John states that the person of the Holy Spirit is the spirit of truth. He is a teacher, He guides us, and He shows us things to come. We can receive the Holy Spirit simply by asking. Jesus said, "Ask and you shall receive the Holy Spirit." When the Holy Spirit is invited into your heart, you will be filled with wonder working power. The Holy Spirit is a comforter that we can rely on.

The Holy Spirit is a teacher of the truth. Receiving the Baptism of the Holy Spirit is very important to having a firm foundation that will cause us to be victorious Christians.

When we become born again, the Holy Spirit places us into the body of Christ. This is the first of three baptisms, the baptism of Salvation spoken of in the Bible *(Acts 2:38-39)*. The second baptism is the baptism of the Holy Spirit **(see** *Acts 19:4-12)*, and Jesus is the one who baptizes with the baptism of the Holy Spirit.

The third baptism spoken of in the Bible is the baptism in water. *(Acts 8:12-14)*, and this is done by the Pastor within the local church.

John 14:17, He is the Spirit of Truth; according to *John 14:26*, He is the Teacher; according to *John 16:13*, He is the one that guides us as believers; and He is the one that gives revelations according to **1 Corinthians 2:6-12**.

The Bible simply says, "...be filled with the Spirit" *(Ephesians 5:18)*. You know that the Bible is God speaking to you. The Word of God is the will of God. It is God's will for you to receive the baptism in the Holy Spirit!

3. How to be filled with the Holy Spirit

Matthew 7:9-13, says... "9 Or what man is there of you, whom if his son ask bread, will he give him a stone? 10 Or if he ask a fish, will he give him a serpent? 11 If ye then, being evil, know how to give good gifts unto your children, how much more shall your Father which is in heaven give good things to them that ask him? 12 Therefore all things whatsoever ye would that men should do to you, do ye even so to them: for this is the law and the prophets. 13 Enter ye in at the strait gate: for wide is the gate, and broad is the way, that leadeth to destruction, and many there be which go in thereat: "

First, we see that you as a son are asking the Father for the Holy Spirit. Even though He has already been given to the church, you are asking and inviting the Holy Spirit to come upon you and endure you with power.

Ask for the Baptism in the Holy Spirit!

We are told that if we ask, we shall receive. The Word assures us that we will receive the best gift--the Holy Spirit and not a counterfeit. Therefore, you may ask expectantly and without fear knowing that your Father gives only good gifts to His children. Jesus said ask and you will receive the Holy Spirit.

Simple Prayer!

> *Lord Jesus, I come to you in faith to receive the Baptism in the Holy Ghost. I ask you to fill me to overflowing with the Holy Spirit the same endowment of power that happened on the Day of Pentecost. Cause rivers of living water to flow out of me as I give utterance to my spiritual language. I receive Him now in Your Name.*

(Now begin to speak in tongues in praise and adoration as the Spirit gives you words.)

Rely on Your Comforter

Jesus called the Holy Spirit the Comforter (**See John 14:16**). The word used for Comforter means counselor, helper, intercessor, advocate, strengthener, and standby.

Learn to rely on the Holy Spirit in all these areas of His ministry. He is the Great Enabler!

Jesus said the Holy Spirit will teach you, not just some things, but ALL the truth. "Ye are of God, little children, and have overcome them: because greater is he that is in you, than he that is in the world" (**1 John 4:4**). Meditate on this verse and confess it with your lips until your spirit sings with the reality that greater is He that is in you than he that is in the world. There is one on the inside to guide you who knows everything from the beginning to the end. Rely on His guidance and direction in every decision.

Expect His power to aid you in every crisis as well as in everyday life. He is more powerful than the enemy--the devil is no match for Him. This Greater One has been instructed to lead you into all the truth. He *will* lead.

We are to be quick to follow. He will not only tell you what to do, but will also help you to do it. He will empower you.

The Holy Spirit that created the universe now dwells in you. Allow your mind to grasp what your spirit is telling you. This Great One lives in you!

After receiving Jesus as our own personal Lord and Savior, the next thing we as Christians are to do is to be filled with the Holy Spirit or receive the Baptism of the Holy Spirit. Again, the reason we need the Baptism of the Holy Spirit has several key things that He does as the third member of the Godhead. From within the Holy Scriptures I will list several of those functions of the person of the Holy Spirit.

He is the Spirit of Truth; He is the *teacher*; He is one that *guides* us as believers; and He is the one that gives *revelations* according and pertaining to the Kingdom of God government. In our yoking up with Jesus and the Kingdom of God Government, we need all that the Holy Spirit has to offer. *(John 14:26; John 16:13)*

> *Acts 2:4, says...* *"⁴And they were all filled with the Holy Ghost, and began to speak with other tongues, as the Spirit gave them utterance."*
>
> *Acts 10:44-46, says...* *"⁴⁴While Peter yet spake these words, the Holy Ghost fell on all them which heard the word. And they of the circumcision which believed were astonished, as many as came with Peter, because that on the Gentiles also was poured out the gift of the Holy Ghost. ⁴⁶For they heard them speak with tongues, and magnify God. Then answered Peter,"*
>
> *Acts 19:6, says...* *"⁶And when Paul had laid his hands upon them, the Holy Ghost came on them; and they spake with tongues, and prophesied."*

In these accounts of believers receiving the Holy Spirit, they began to speak with other tongues. Nowhere in the New Testament does it say the Holy Spirit does the speaking.

The believer speaks as the Holy Spirit gives them utterance. You must supply the sound as the Holy Spirit supplies the words. These words will be unknown to you. The Scripture teaches us that in the spirit, we speak mysteries unto God.

> *1 Corinthians 14:2, says...* *"²For he that speaketh in an unknown tongue speaketh not unto men, but unto God: for no man understandeth him; howbeit in the spirit he speaketh mysteries."*

One translation says we speak divine secrets. You can pray beyond your natural knowledge when you pray in other tongues.

The Holy Spirit comes to our aid and bears us up in our weakness, for we do not know what prayer to offer nor how to offer it worthily as we ought. The Holy Spirit Himself goes to meet our supplication and pleads in our behalf with unspeakable yearning and groaning too deep for utterance.

He who searches the hearts of men knows what is in the mind of God the Father--what His intent is because the Spirit intercedes and pleads [before God] on behalf of the saints according to and in harmony with God's will. **(See Romans 8:26-27, the Amplified Bible)**

The Holy Spirit comes to our aid to help us in prayer when we do not know how to pray as we ought and gives us utterance in other tongues, praying the perfect will of God. We need this help. So much of the time, we know so little. We may only see a symptom of a much deeper problem.

The Holy Spirit goes right to the root of the problem and prays the perfect will of God for us. In looking at *Jude 1:20*, the Amplified Bible says, "...But you, beloved, build yourselves up [founded] on your most holy faith--make progress, rise like an edifice higher and higher praying in the Holy Spirit." Praying in tongues edifies you.

This means to build up or charge as we charge a battery. I am so grateful to be able to pray in the Holy Spirit. In the scripture when believers received the baptism in the Holy Spirit, they spoke with other tongues. This will be a great blessing to you. After you receive your prayer language, pray in the spirit every day. This helps your spirit to be strong and keeps rule over your life.

> ***1 Corinthians 14:14, says...*** *"14For if I pray in an unknown tongue, my spirit prayeth, but my understanding is unfruitful."*

The Amplified Bible says, "... my spirit [by the Holy Spirit within me] prays..." The Holy Spirit is giving your spirit the prayer or praise. Your voice is giving sound to this spiritual language.

The Amplified Bible says that Cornelius and his household talked in unknown languages and extolled and magnified God. The definition of extol is to praise enthusiastically.

You will receive the indwelling of the Holy Spirit and your spirit will immediately have a desire to express itself in praise to God.

How could you help but pour forth praise after having the Holy Spirit, who proceeds directly from the Father God, come upon you in power? Your well begins to overflow and rivers are the result (*John 4:14, 7:37-39*)! Spiritual blessings are received by faith--not by sight or by feeling. Your lips may flutter and your tongue feels thick or you may hear the supernatural words forming down inside your being.

None of the above may be evident. The lips and tongue are the organs we use to form words.

Your physical instruments of speech lips, tongues, and vocal cords must cooperate with your spirit in order to give sound to prayer or praise that the Holy Spirit has given. Immediately upon receiving, spiritual language is ready for you to speak.

Remember, you have nothing to fear. God has already said that you would receive the real thing. *Isaiah 57:19* tells us that God created the fruit of the lips. Do not be concerned with what it sounds like to you.

God will perfect your praise. "...Out of the mouth of babes and suckling's thou hast perfected praise."

> *Matthew 21:16, says...* "*16 And said unto him, Hearest thou what these say? And Jesus saith unto them, Yea; have ye never read, Out of the mouth of babes and suckling's thou hast perfected praise?*"
>
> *Mark 16:17, says...* "*17And these signs shall follow them that believe; In my name shall they cast out devils; they shall speak with new tongues;*"

When you pray in tongues, you are praying in the spirit. Just as your native language, such as English, is the voice of your mind, praying in tongues is the voice of your spirit.

Therefore, after you ask, speak no more of your native language. You cannot speak two languages at once.

4. What should I expect?

Let us look at accounts in the book of Acts that describe believers being filled with the Spirit. What do these verses say happened when the New Testament believer received the Holy Spirit?

> ***Acts 2:4 says...*** *"⁴And they were all filled with the Holy Ghost, and began to speak with other tongues, as the Spirit gave them utterance."*
>
> ***Acts 10:44-46, says...*** *"⁴⁴While Peter yet spake these words, the Holy Ghost fell on all them which heard the word. And they of the circumcision which believed were astonished, as many as came with Peter, because that on the*
>
> *Gentiles also was poured out the gift of the Holy Ghost. ⁴⁶For they heard them speak with tongues, and magnify God. Then answered Peter,"*
>
> ***Acts 19:6, says...*** *"⁶And when Paul had laid his hands upon them, the Holy Ghost came on them; and they spake with tongues, and prophesied."*

Expect the Holy Spirit to come upon you just as He came upon the believers on the Day of Pentecost, at Samaria, at Cornelius' home, and at Ephesus. You will begin to speak in other tongues as the Spirit gives you the words.

5. Different kinds of tongues

To the natural mind, speaking in tongues may seem silly. However, as you study the Word of God on this subject, you will see the great benefits of praying in tongues. Let us look at the Word of God.

> *1 Corinthians 12:10, says...* "*¹⁰ To another the working of miracles; to another prophecy; to another discerning of spirits; to another divers kinds of tongues; to another the interpretation of tongues:*"
>
> *1 Corinthians 12:28, says...* "*²⁸ And God hath set some in the church, first apostles, secondarily prophets, thirdly teachers, after that miracles, then gifts of healings, helps, governments, diversities of tongues.*
>
> *1 Corinthians 13:1, says...* "*¹³Though I speak with the tongues of men and of angels, and have not charity, I am become as sounding brass, or a tinkling cymbal.*"
>
> *1 Corinthians 14:2, says...* ²*For he that speaketh in an unknown tongue speaketh not unto men, but unto God: for no man understandeth him; howbeit in the spirit he speaketh mysteries.*

What is the purpose of speaking in tongues? The purpose for speaking in tongues that we can see from the Word of God is the gift of tongues requires interpretation. This might be called public manifestation. This manifestation is used, as the apostle Paul said, for ministry "in the church."

Another purpose for speaking in tongues might be called the private manifestation, and does not necessarily require an interpretation. This manifestation is available for every believer, as the apostle Paul said, "to edify himself."

6. What are the benefits of speaking in tongues?

A. Have you ever wanted to *praise the Lord from your innermost being?* Have you ever wanted to thank God for all He has done for you? Have you ever wanted to talk to God "heart to heart," but you could not seem to find the right words?

Sometime our English language is so limited when we want to praise, thank, or talk to the Lord. The Holy Spirit helps us talk to God from heart to heart through speaking in tongues.

B. Speaking in tongues is also called "a prayer language," or "praying or speaking in the Spirit." When we exercise this prayer language, we are literally bypassing our mind and intellect, and we are praying straight from our spirit to God (see *1 Corinthians 14:2*).

Speaking to God in our prayer language is like having a *direct hotline to God*, and our prayer or speech is not clouded by our thoughts, emotions, or feelings.

As we pray in the Spirit in tongues, we receive a great spiritual blessing. **(See *1 Corinthians 14:4*)**

C. Praying in the Holy Spirit is the help that we need when we do not know how to pray.

D. Praying in the Holy Spirit is one of the best habits you can get into early in your Christian life — that is, praying in the Holy Ghost.

Praying in tongues, not as a mindless exercise but with the awareness that as you pray in tongues you are literally charging up your spirit and *building yourself up on your most holy faith.* **(See *Jude 20*).**

E. Receive Strategy from the Holy Spirit - Many times, when speaking about the person of the Holy Spirit, our attention is immediately focused on the person speaking in tongues. The reason for this is because the devil is attacking so many people and trying to sway them from receiving the person of the Holy Spirit. The devil has us in a state of confusion concerning speaking in tongues.

There are many other things that the person of the Holy Spirit has to offer than just the ability to speak in tongues.

After all, He is the third member of the Godhead. His primary responsibility is to lead, guide, and teach the body of Christ (believers/church) about the things concerning the Kingdom of God.

It is our responsibility to cooperate (partner) with Him. Remember, the Holy Spirit is the one that empowered Jesus during His earthly ministry.

Beginning with the baptism of water, Jesus received the baptism of the Holy Spirit as recorded in *John 1:31-34*.

From this point, the Holy Spirit led and guided Jesus concerning His earthly ministry. The first victory of Jesus was when the Holy Spirit led Him into the wilderness and enabled Jesus to defeat the devil during His time of temptation.

As we examine the book of *Acts 10:38*, we will find the significance of the person of the Holy Spirit in Jesus' life, and He the person of the Holy Spirit desires to be that significant person in our lives if we will cooperate (partner) with Him.

F. Let us look at several examples in the book of Acts, which is the Acts of the Holy Spirit through the Apostles.

1). We have Phillip who was a deacon in *Acts 6;* an evangelist in *Acts 8:29;* being instructed by an angel who was sent by the person of the Holy Spirit to join himself to the chariot to lead the Ethiopian Eunuch to salvation. Then we see the Holy Spirit translating Philip to Azotus.

2). We have the Apostle Peter in *Acts 10*, the Acts of person of the Holy Spirit through the Apostle Peter in leading Cornelius and his household to salvation. Initially, it began with Cornelius praying and the person of the Holy Spirit sends an angel to Cornelius' prayer chamber giving him instruction via an angel to send for Peter (*Acts 10:7*). In *Acts 10:20*, we see where Apostle Peter has a vision that was given unto him by the Holy Spirit instructing; "Go with them doubting nothing for I have sent them."

3). We have Acts of the person of the Holy Spirit in the life of the Apostle Paul. In *Acts 16:6*, we see the Apostle Paul entertaining the idea of going into Galatia but was forbidden by the person of the Holy Spirit.

The Holy Spirit gave Paul a vision in *Acts 16:9* revealing that his help was needed in Macedonia. So here we see the Apostle Paul receiving specific direction.

As we have seen from these three examples, the person of the Holy Spirit will lead and guide you.

He will give you strategy for what you are supposed to do concerning the Kingdom of God.

Remember that He is the third member of the Godhead. He is our helper and we should look to Him for guidance and strategies concerning every area of our life here on earth. These are not just spiritual things but the natural area as well (*Romans 8:14*).

We have many examples of strategies given by the Holy Spirit in the Bible. Let us examine this example in **2 Kings 4:1-7**.

What did a certain woman do? Now there cried a certain woman of the wives of the sons of the prophets unto Elisha, saying, Thy servant my husband is dead; and thou knowest that thy servant did fear the Lord and the creditor is come to take unto him my two sons to be bondsmen.

1. **What did the man of God do?** And Elisha said unto her, what shall I do for thee? Tell me, what hast thou in the house?

2. What was the answer given by a certain woman? Thine handmaid hath not anything in the house, save a pot of oil.

3. What did the man of God do? The Holy Spirit through the man of God said… Go, borrow thee vessels abroad of all thy neighbors, *even* empty vessels; borrow not a few. And when thou art come in, thou shalt shut the door upon thee, and upon thy sons, and shalt pour out into all those vessels, and thou shalt set aside that which is full.

4. What did a certain woman do? Therefore, she went from him, and shut the door upon her and upon her sons, who brought *the vessels* to her; and she poured out. It came to pass, when the vessels were full, that she said unto her son, Bring me yet a vessel. He said unto her, *there is* not a vessel more. The oil stayed. Then she came and told the man of God (miracle of increase of oil).

5. **What did the Holy Spirit do by His power through the man of God?** The Holy Spirit said through the man of God, Go, sell the oil, and PAY THY DEBT, and live (this means that she had more than enough to pay her bills) thou and thy children of the rest (2 Kings 4:7 *Emphasis added*).

Summary

While Jesus walked the earth, the Holy Spirit was in Him. However, Jesus' physical body was limited to one location, so the effectiveness of the Holy Spirit was limited.

Today, through the body of Christ, the Holy Spirit can saturate the whole earth. When the Holy Spirit came into the earth after Jesus' ascension, He set up residence inside of every believer. Once we are born again, the Comforter lives inside us.

We come into the Kingdom of God, and at the same time, the Kingdom of God comes inside of us. As believers, we have the whole Kingdom of God inside of us. God's plan is for the Kingdom of God to spread throughout the entire earth through the body of Christ.

John 14:12, 16, says… *"¹²Verily, verily, I say unto you, He that believeth on me, the works that I do shall he do also; and greater works than these shall he do; because I go unto my Father. "¹⁶ And I will pray the Father, and he shall give you another Comforter, that he may abide with you forever;"*

Jesus was saying that we could do the works He did and greater works, or more works, by the Holy Spirit coming to live inside many believers. The Holy Spirit made the whole kingdom available to all who would believe on Jesus. As believers, we now have the kingdom in us and through us the Holy Spirit will cause the kingdom to manifest on earth as it is in heaven. One must first be born again and then one must receive the Baptism of the Holy Spirit.

The person of the Holy Spirit is available to all of us. Once you are filled with the Holy Spirit, you will find that is all you really need, when the Holy Spirit lives inside of you; He will teach you all that is true, and He will guide you in the right direction. Depend on Him in all aspects of your life; allow Him to instruct you, to lead you, and you can rest assured that you will never be led astray, but give you divine strategies.

Chapter 5
Kingdom System of Communication

In examining scriptures, I look for references that pertain to Heavenly Communication. Over the years of being a Christian, I have purposely set my heart to obey the Word of God and the Spirit of God. As I continue my study of "In Understanding the Kingdom of God," and especially the subject of Heaven, I have found it to be so rewarding that God loves us beyond our wildest imaginations. Even the various means of communication are so cool. The very first miracle that Jesus performed was the miracle of pleasure by turning the water into wine. **(See *John* 2:3-9)**

Various Ways of Communication

In the Kingdom of God, which is the Government of God, we have various ways of communicating.

Yes, we will be able to talk as we do here on earth using our vocabulary, which we speak audibly, but I also believe that our vocabulary will be even greater than ever before once we get to Heaven.

The highest level of communicating that I discovered from reading the Word of God and reading after those people who have visited Heaven, is that when they have questions, they will obtain an answer immediately before they have a chance to ask their questions.

> *Matthew 6:8; "Be not ye therefore like unto them: for your Father knoweth what things ye have need of, before ye ask him."*

The reason that we need to ask while here on earth is because it gives God a legal right to move on our behalf. **(See Amos 3:7, Psalms 115:16)**

Again, I believe the primary reason for an audible vocabulary is so we can speak decrees and make declarations of what we want to come to pass.

During Jesus' earthly ministry He taught about the person of the Holy Spirit and His role in the life of believers after His departure from earth and his return to the third Heaven. You might say what does this have to do with communication in Heaven? As Dr. Roger Mills would say Jesus said to him, "look, listen, and learn."

A. **Jesse Duplantis** - In his book, "Close Encounter of the God Kind," said in speaking with Jesus, a thought (question) would come into his mind and before he could speak it, Jesus would answer him.⁵

B. **Bishop Earthquake Kelley** - In his book, *"Bound to Lose Destined to Win,"* Bishop Kelly said he heard a voice say, "You're wondering who those children are." It was clear that this voice was responding to his thoughts. Bishop Kelly was surprised that someone could read his thoughts. He looked around and although he didn't see anybody, he knew that he was hearing the voice of the Lord (Dec. 7, 1998 / 2006).

C. **Freddy Vest** - A rodeo cowboy said during an interview on the *700 Club* that he had a heart attack while sitting on the back of his horse. He also remembers having conversations with God. "When he was there, there was communication, but the communication was inside of Freddy and it was nothing that verbally you would have ears to hear or a mouth to speak it."¹⁸

Jesus taught about the person of the Holy Spirit, and His role in the life of the believers after His departure from earth and return to the third Heaven.

> *John 14:16-17, 26;* ¹⁷<u>He dwelleth with you, and shall be in you.</u> ²⁶ <u>He shall teach you all things.</u>

In order to understand the makeup of mankind, there are several scriptures that we need to know that will help us in this area. The makeup of mankind:

> *2 Corinthians 4:16* - "<u>outward man</u> and <u>inward man</u>
>
> *1 Peter 3:4* - "But let it be the <u>hidden man</u> of the heart
>
> *1 Thessalonians 5:23* - "Your <u>whole spirit and soul and body</u>

As we examine the Holy Scriptures, we see that Man is a spirit, has a soul that is comprised of (mind, will, emotion, and imagination), and lives in a body.

> *2 Peter 1:13-14* - "this tabernacle (physical house)
>
> *Colossians 1:13* - but at the same time the Kingdom of God come on the inside of our spirit via the Holy Spirit, and He is living within our spirit *(Luke 17:21, Romans 8:11; 14-16).*

1) **The Inward Witness** – On the inside of each one of us, we have a God tool called *sensor mechanism* that can be referred to as a "check red-light, stop signal." It is not a voice that says do not do this or that, it is an *inward intuition*.

When you have a velvety-like feeling in your spirit, it is the witness of the Spirit to go-- the green light to go ahead signal. Through the Inward witness, the Holy Spirit will guide in all the affairs of life, not just spiritual but natural also.

The Inward witness is just as supernatural as guidance through vision and so on. It is just not as spectacular. Many people are looking for the spectacular and missing the supernatural that is right there all the time. **(See Romans 8:16)**

2) **The Inward Voice** *Romans 9:1* "still small voice" - The Inward man, who is a Spirit man, has a voice-- just as the outward man has a voice. We call this voice our conscience. Your spirit has a voice. Your spirit will speak to you. The still small voice is the voice of our own spirit speaking.

You see our spirit picks it up from the Holy Spirit who is in us. Again, that still small voice, that Inward voice, not authoritative, just something on the inside of me that I am going to do such and such. **(See *Elijah, 1 King 19:12*)**

3) **The Voice of the Holy Spirit *Acts 10:19-20*** - When the Holy Spirit within you speaks, it is more "authoritative." Although He is inside of you, you look around to see who said it.

You think somebody behind you said something. Then you realize it was coming from the inside of you. **(See *1 Samuel 3:1-19*)**

Communications through Visions

Visions - Sometimes God leads us through visions. There are three kinds of visions: spiritual vision, trances, and open visions. In a spiritual vision, you see with the eyes of your spirit – not with your physical eyes.

4) Spiritual Visions - Caesarea called Cornelius, a centurion of what was called the Italian Regiment, ²a devout *man* and one who feared God with all his household, who gave alms generously to the people, and prayed to God always. ³About the ninth hour of the day he saw clearly in a vision an angel of God coming in and saying to him, "Cornelius!" (*Acts 10:1-3 NKJV*).

Cornelius was a devout man, but he was not born again. He did not know Jesus because he was a Jewish proselyte.

The angel who appeared to him in a vision could not preach the gospel to him. God did not call angels to preach the gospel; however, the angel did tell Cornelius where to send for someone who could preach the gospel to him and tell him how to be saved.

The scripture calls the Cornelius' experience a vision *(Acts 10:3)*. It was a spiritual vision. Cornelius saw in the spirit world, and there are angels out there in the spirit world.

If others had been present, they would not have seen anything. Yet if the angel had taken on a visible form, anyone could have seen it. *(See Hebrews 13:2)*

The second type of vision is when a person falls into a trance. Cornelius did not fall into a trance – Peter did.

5) Trance Visions - In *Acts 10:9-11*, "The next day, as they went on their journey and drew near the city, Peter went up on the housetop to pray, about the sixth hour. 10 Then he became very hungry and wanted to eat; but while they made ready, he fell into a trance 11 and saw heaven opened, and an object like a great sheet bound at the four corners, descending to him and let down to the earth. *(See Acts 10:9-11 NKJV)*

When one falls into a trance, his physical senses are suspended; you do not know where you are at the moment. You are not unconscious, but you do not know what is going on around you. You are more conscious of spiritual things than physical things.

The third type of vision is called an open vision. Your physical senses are intact. Your eyes are wide open, and you are aware of what is going on around you. You are not in a trance.

6) Open Vision - In *Acts 8:26-29*, "Now an angel of the Lord spoke to Philip, saying, "Arise and go toward the south along the road which goes down from Jerusalem to Gaza." This is desert. ^{27}So he arose and went. And, behold, a man of Ethiopia, a eunuch of great authority under Candace the Queen of the Ethiopians, who had charge of all her treasury, and had come to Jerusalem to worship,^{28}was returning. And sitting in his chariot, he was reading Isaiah the prophet.^{29}Then the Spirit said to Philip, "Go near, and overtake this chariot" *Acts 8:26-29* (NKJV).

Philip's eyes were wide open. He saw the angel talking to him. He knew exactly where he was and he knew what was going on around him.

As you can see, heavenly communications have not changed. As we read about the various means of communication in the Bible, we will see it is the Bible that unravels things about heaven that we should be familiar with.

While here on earth, we will communicate via our vocabulary speaking audibly. As Christians we have the Holy Spirit speaking to us via our spirit, and we have our minds. In the mind area, we have thoughts coming from more than one source so we cannot just accept every thought that drifts into our minds. We must examine them in light of God's Word, and only then are we to receive those thoughts and act upon them.

Again, I believe the primary reason for an audible vocabulary is so we can speak decrees, and make declarations of what we want to come to pass.

We have the "Inward witness, the still small voice of our human spirit, the authority voice of the Holy Spirit, spiritual vision, trances, and open vision.

As a Christian, we learn to discern between the two sources of thoughts. We are instructed to cast down the evil thoughts, while receiving the good thoughts of God. **(See *Romans 12:1, 2; 2 Corinthians 10:5*)**

In Heaven, we can flow in the highest level of communicating by just receiving from God and flowing with Him. Jesse Duplantis (as mentioned before) in speaking with Jesus, a thought (question) would come into his mind, and before Jesse could speak it, Jesus would answer him.[5]

Summary

If we are in tune with the Spirit of God, we would beware of the impending dangerous acts that are about to happen that are being caused by the kingdom of darkness.

In understanding Heavenly Communication, it will help to protect us from the cowardly act of the devil and his cohorts. Please know whatever you are doing that is not under the direct command of God via the Holy Spirit, verified by the Word of God, is out of the will of God.

Therefore, you DO NOT have his guarantee of divine protection or blessing upon what you are doing. As we see that the Son of God could do nothing of Himself, what make us think that we can do things ourselves separate from the Kingdom of God outside the leading of the Holy Spirit? If there was ever a time in which we must cooperate with the Holy Spirit it is now. I want to encourage you not to limit this to your personal life; I am talking in ministry, in church services, on your job, etc.

The essence of this message is that whatever you are about to do as a Christian in co-laboring with God, you must operate in obedience to the voice of God verified by the Word of God. If this is not the case, whatever you are doing or about to do is not in obedience to God, and it will be considered dead works.

The Holy Spirit is abiding in our spirits and communicates with us through our spirits, not through our minds. The way your spirit knows things, your head does not know. We have been taught to listen our heads and have never been taught to listen to our spirits, and we are reluctant to do so.

The reason that spirit-filled believers continually miss is because our spirits which should guide us are kept locked away in prison so to speak. Knowledge or intellect has taken the throne. *(Proverbs 20:27)* and *Proverbs 3:5-6* "<u>acknowledge</u> him, and he shall direct thy paths." Are you being led by the Holy Spirit or are you being led by circumstances, situations, and emotions? If you are not being led by the Holy Spirit, you will not know how close we are to the coming of the Lord Jesus Christ. **(See Romans 8:14-16).**

What would it be like if every thought that crossed your mind was blasted on a loud speaker in Heaven? We must renew our minds while on earth, and we will reach perfection in Heaven.

Chapter 6
the Kingdom of God Ambassador

The New Testament has material about being an ambassador. The apostle Paul realized this more than any other disciple of Jesus. His zeal, knowledge, activity, and sacrifice set him apart as an exceptional example of Christian living.

> *2 Corinthians 5:17-19* "Therefore, if anyone is in Christ, he is a new creation; old things have passed away; behold, all things have become new. Now all things are of God, who has reconciled us to Himself through Jesus Christ, and has given us the ministry of reconciliation, that is, that God was in Christ reconciling the world to Himself, not imputing their trespasses to them, and has committed to us the word of reconciliation."

> *2 Corinthians 5:20-21* "Now then, we are <u>ambassadors</u> for Christ, as though God were pleading through us: we implore you on Christ's behalf, be reconciled to God. For He made Him who knew no sin to be sin for us, that we might become the righteousness of God in Him.

Paul's love and devotion to fellow members of the body of Christ is a template for all who follow Jesus. Paul's public ministry was the key that unlocked a great gathering of elect from among the Gentiles. Paul's exemplary ambassadorship of the heavenly kingdom, as well as his instruction to the early church, is finely detailed in the book of Acts.

An "ambassador" in the dictionary means a diplomatic official of the highest rank sent by a government to represent it on a temporary mission, as for negotiating a treaty or matters. In the spiritual realm, the name of the "spiritual diplomatic representative" is an ambassador for Christ.

As faithful, on-fire, pure-hearted believers in Jesus Christ, we will have the necessary character-qualities that will qualify us to be trustworthy ambassadors.

Not for an earthly kingdom or government, but for God's eternal purposes concerning His Kingdom. Why? So that people are reconciled to God, they are saved from their sins and they "might become the righteousness of God in Him."

The word apostle means "one sent forth." Synonyms might be representative or delegate and even ambassador. Paul referred to himself as an "ambassador in chains". *(See Ephesians 6:20)*

This is hardly the view we take of diplomatic ambassadors today. But Paul does not say this to elicit pity. Rather he tells the church not to lose heart over what he is suffering because it is for the church's glory. Truly, he was a great ambassador!

Consequently, we can learn from Paul's wonderful example of ambassadorship and demonstrate, as he did, a ministry of reconciliation now. Our Christ-like behavior in this world brings a certain amount of help and healing to a world that needs deliverance. "A wicked messenger falleth into mischief: but a faithful ambassador *is* health" *(Proverbs 13:17)*.

In biblical days, the role of an ambassador was somewhat different than today, and more critical due to different communication methods.

Today an ambassador can contact his country with urgent questions or vital issues and receive quick instruction on critical matters.

In ancient times, however, an ambassador made decisions by himself. Consequently, the selection of an ambassador by a king had to be done with great care. The candidate had to know well the mind and heart of his ruler.

He had to know the plans and purposes of his king. He had to be skillful in presenting himself as though he was the monarch himself.

The ultimate purpose of an ambassador in any day is to foster a good relationship between the government representatives and the people of the host country and its rulers. Importantly, an ambassador is a citizen of another country. Paul made this clear in his own case and for those who are accepted of God and begotten of the holy spirit, "For our conversation is in heaven; from whence also we look for the Savior, the Lord Jesus Christ. *(Philippians 3:20);*

"Who hath delivered us from the power of darkness, and hath translated us into the kingdom of his dear Son." **(Colossians 1:13)**

Paul in his world represented God and Christ in his world. Both his words and actions in the presence of rulers and ordinary people reflected those of his heavenly kingdom. His pastoral counsel brought untold numbers into a relationship with God through Christ Jesus. Consider the characteristics of an ideal ambassador and how Paul reflected them in his ministry.

Qualifications of an Ambassador

Before you ever become an ambassador for God, you must know the kingdom of Heaven, and the Kingdom of God. You most have knowledge of its forces, its might, its armour, and its universal position *(Hebrews 12:22-23, 13:14, Revelation 21:10-24).* God will not let you represent His kingdom until you know His kingdom. This requires study and experience. To be an ambassador in the Kingdom of God requires a personal knowledge of the king (Jesus).

An ambassador must have credentials. This tells us that we have to be called to be an ambassador, prepared to be an ambassador, and sent forth with a commission by God as an ambassador.

You cannot decide on your own. As an ambassador you must be received by the people to whom you are sent. There must be agreement between the two nations.

Too many Christians never wait until they are endowed with power. Paul says, "Ye are my epistles." It is important that the ambassador who represents Christ be filled with Christ's word, fruits, and gifts. An ambassador has authority. He is under the authority of his government, yet he has the authority of that government.

An ambassador must know the principles of authority. He has a rule or a covering over him, which is his government.

These same principles apply to the ambassadors of the Kingdom of God. If we are not under the covering of a church body, we will get into trouble.

Every ambassador in the Kingdom of God must submit to those who rule over *him (John 1:12, Mark 3:14, Romans10:9-10, Psalm 149:7, Matthew 28:18,* and *Hebrew 13:7, 17)*. These verses speak of authority. We must remember that an ambassador speaks with authority because he is speaking the words of his government. He speaks with faith and with wisdom.

An ambassador has a task. It is not to move among the common people. He moves in "high places" with governments. An ambassador in the Kingdom of God also deals with governments, principalities, and powers *(Ephesians 6:12)*. He wrestles and binds the strong, he deals with Satan's highest authorities, and brings the devil's authorities into line. An ambassador must be prepared to stand alone against the will of the devil's kingdom. He is there representing the Kingdom of God. He must confront seducing spirits and false doctrines. He contends for the faith of the Kingdom of God.

An ambassador listens carefully to both those in his host country and his own country to fully understand their needs and situations. When there is conflict or disagreement, he will seek to bring about mutual understanding. Even as a prisoner Paul's patience marked his demeanour and submission to providential experiences. Paul in his dealings with rulers sought to bring about mutual understanding concerning the truth.

This is no small thing! Do we get this?

I mean, do we actually realize what an honour it is to serve the Lord Jesus Christ as His ambassador--the highest-ranking spiritual representative! Being an ambassador is a high calling. He is often a mediator, a peacemaker, and committed to the word of reconciliation.

Can you meet these standards?

- Do you know the Kingdom of God? Are you able to deal with the wicked powers of the kingdom of darkness?
- Do you understand the message of the Kingdom of God and can you present that message with wisdom and convincing power?
- Are you under authority?

- Do you have authority?
- Have you prepared yourself with prayer and study?
- Has the Lord commissioned you?

Summary

Sometimes we must face some hard questions as to our motives in wanting to be an ambassador since everything is provided for the ambassador. He does not worry for his provision, for his family, and even for his debts if he has any. Before he is sent out, the government makes sure that his debt is cleared out. Because once the people of another country where he would be assigned learn that he has an outstanding debt, the reputation of the one who sent him will be tarnished.

The ambassador is never affected by an economic crisis where he is assigned because his provision does not come from that place but from the country that sent him. It is the same with the ambassador of heaven--he does not have to worry about the economic crisis on earth because the provision does not come from here but from heaven. Thus, the ambassador is a worry free person, a fearless person, and a person full of confidence.

Chapter 7
What is the Church?
How is the church connect to the Kingdom of God?

The word church is the ecclesia and this has to do with the called out ones. This is talking about the governmental body of Christ, not a religion or a religious group of people.

Let me explain. Here in the United States, we have what is called the State of the Union Address. This address is presented by the President of the United States to a joint session of the United States Congress. The address not only reports on the condition of the nation, but also allows the President to outline his legislative agenda for which the President needs the cooperation of the Congress as he establishes national priorities.

The address fulfills the rules in Article II of the United States Constitution, Section 3. It requires the President to give Congress information on the "state of the union" and recommends any measures that he believes are necessary and expedient. This governmental body comes together to make and ratify laws. Various representatives go back to their district to inform their constituents of these laws.

This is what Jesus is speaking of as He prophetically speaks about the Church. He is going to build His church, a governmental body of believers who were chosen before the foundation of the world. Similar to the congressional body of the United States, the Church is the legislative body of the government of God.

When we come together in a local church building, we receive instructions via the fivefold ministry--the Executive members of the body of Christ.

> *According to Ephesians 4:11-14 (NLT), "11 Now these are the gifts Christ gave to the church: the apostles, the prophets, the evangelists, and the pastors and teachers. 12 Their responsibility is to equip God's people to do his work and build up the church, the body of Christ. 13 This will continue until we all come to such unity in our faith and knowledge of God's Son that we will be mature in the Lord, measuring up to the full and complete standard of Christ. 14 Then we will no longer be immature like children. We will not be tossed and blown about by every wind of new teaching. We will not be influenced when people try to trick us with lies so clever they sound like the truth."*

The person of the Holy Spirit give gifts. They include revelation gifts which are the word of wisdom, the word of knowledge, and the discerning of spirits; power gifts which are the gift of faith, the gift of healings, and the gift of working of miracles; and the gifts of utterance which are the gift of prophecy, the gift of tongues, and the gift of interpretation.

Here are the ministry gifts to the church according to *Ephesians 4:8, 11-13:*

- **Apostle** – Outstanding spiritual gifts – Deep personal experience, power, and ability to establish churches. Able to provide adequate spiritual leadership.
- **Prophet** – A prophet is one who has visions and revelation. Word of wisdom, word of knowledge, or discerning of spirits on a consistent manifestation (Ghazi).
- **Evangelist** – The working of miracles and gifts of healings. The evangelist's ministry is more of a roving ministry.

- **Pastor** – A pastor should have the revelation gifts and the utterance gifts. Pastoring is supernatural. He usually lives in the locality of the sheep.

- **Teacher** – The teaching ministry requires a divine gift. This ministry's power comes by the Holy Spirit and is not dry. It conveys rivers of living water, *Romans 8:13-16;* the leading of the Holy Spirit in your own personal life (*John 14:17, 1 Corinthians 6:19*).

The fivefold ministry gifts were never given to replace your personal relationship with God, but to help confirm the things that God has revealed to us personally via the Holy Spirit. After coming together to praise and worship God, then the believers should go back to their sphere or area of influence (family, work, etc.) and share what they have been instructed to do.

Overall, this is not being done but rather we are preaching and teaching church and not teaching the Kingdom of God.

If you check the four gospels and the first chapter of the book of Acts, it will help you to understand that Jesus spoke about the Kingdom of God and prophesied about it as the government of God.

Also, remember in *Matthew 4:17* Jesus announced that "the Kingdom of Heaven is at hand" and in order to become a citizen of heaven you must be born into the Kingdom of God. We covered this in a previous paragraph.

The church (ecclesia), the legislative governmental body of Christ, has a two-legged agenda based upon *Matthew 28:18-20, Mark 16:15-18*:

1. *Matthew 28:18-20* - They were to go out and make disciples.

2. *Mark 16:15 –18* - They were to create kingdom culture. In other words, when your local assembly of believers come together they should look like heaven on earth. There should be worshipping, praising, rejoicing, and shouting. There should be people from all nationalities. For the Kingdom of God is not meat and drink; but righteousness, and peace, and joy in the Holy Ghost (*Romans 14:17*).

The culture of the Kingdom of God is more real, more powerful, and more enticing to those who are lost in the world culture.

When we as Christians (kingdom citizens) come together, we come together as the legislative body of the government of God. We have been anointed to carry the mantle of authority wherever we go. When we see the devil and the cohort of the kingdom of darkness, he is trying to do things contrary to the will of God.

We have the authority to stop it but most Christians (kingdom citizens) are focused on being religious and not functioning as kingdom citizens who use their authority to bring things in line with the Kingdom of God (**see *Genesis 2:15*,** "to dress and keep it").

In the sovereign Kingdom of God, there is no voting. You hear the Gospel of the Kingdom of God dictated by the King and it is your responsibility to carry it out. A King does not ask for things, He decrees it! As Christians (kingdom citizens), we are under a constitution or covenant of the rulership of King.

To be a Christian (kingdom citizen) is a pleasure. The king is obligated to care for the welfare of his citizens (**see** ***Philippians 4:19***).

Also, wherever we go as Christians (kingdom citizens), we are to bring into the Kingdom of God culture, peace, joy, prosperity, health, etc. (**see** ***Psalm 103:1-5***). The number one responsibility of the Christian (kingdom citizen) is to submit to the King. As a Christian (kingdom citizen), we are rewarded for obedience. This is a guarantee that we will enjoy all the benefits of the kingdom.

As the Holy Spirit is the governing body of Christ, we need to understand the church is a living organism, not the four walls of a building. The true believers within the walls are the called out ones, (Greek word ecclesia). We have executive leaders such as apostles, prophets, evangelists, pastors, and teachers.

These leaders receive instructions from headquarters, where the Lord Jesus Christ is seated at the right hand of the throne of God in Heaven via the Holy Spirit.

These executive leaders then impart revelation knowledge received from Heaven to the citizens of the Kingdom of Heaven by preaching and teaching via the Holy Spirit.

Also, individuals can receive confirmation of what they have received because individuals can receive from headquarters just like the executive leaders can via the person of the Holy Spirit. This impartation and confirmation helps us to be effective citizens of the Kingdom of God.

As members of the body of Christ and citizens of the Kingdom of God, when we come together for Kingdom business, the purpose is threefold:

- To bestow upon our God, our King, and Holy Spirit the praise and worship that the Godhead is so worthy to receive, thus creating an atmosphere.

- To receive specific instructions about Kingdom operations for this embassy to carry out.

- As ambassadors of the Kingdom of God, we are to receive instructions and directions.

Then we are to examine the constitution to see if what we have received is in line with the Word of God. As citizens, we are to disseminate to each of our jurisdictions (places of influence) executing these instructions and directions as examples.

Consequently, we become effective kingdom citizens through our living a Kingdom of God life.

This is similar to the government of the United States. We have elected officials that come from each state to a central location (Washington, DC) to conduct government business making laws on behalf of the citizens.

Then the elected officials will go back to his/her district, state, or jurisdiction that they represent and inform them of the laws that have been made.

Here is an example of the functionality of a king in a kingdom:

> *According to **Luke 23:1-7**, "¹And the whole multitude of them arose, and led Him unto Pilate. ²And they began to accuse Him, saying, we found this fellow perverting the nation, and forbidding to give tribute to Caesar, saying that he himself is Christ a King. ³And Pilate asked Him, saying, Art thou the king of the Jews? And he answered him and said, Thou sayest it.*

> *⁴Then said Pilate to the chief priests and to the people, I find no fault in this man. ⁵And they were the more fierce, saying, He stirreth up the people, teaching throughout all Jewry, beginning from Galilee to this place. ⁶When Pilate heard of Galilee, he asked whether the man was a Galilean. ⁷And as soon as he knew that he belonged unto Herod's jurisdiction, he sent Him to Herod who himself also was at Jerusalem at that time."*

What is a Jurisdiction?

It means the range of authority that a King has and that he has the final say over that domain or territory. What does this mean to us as kingdom citizens? It means that wherever we go in direct obedience to where King Jesus has sent us we must do kingdom business on His behalf.

As the sole of our feet tread, it will become kingdom jurisdiction and as a Christian (kingdom citizen), we have the final word over that domain or territory. The Jews took Jesus to the one that was in authority, King Pilate, because he had authority in that jurisdiction.

When King Pilate found out that Jesus was a Galilean, he sent Jesus to King Herod because Galilee was part of his jurisdiction.

We can see from these scriptures that a picture is being painted so that we as kingdom citizens can see the function of a kingdom.

As the Holy Spirit is the governing body of Christ, we need to understand the church is a living organism, not the four walls.

The true believers within the walls are the called out ones, (Greek word Ecclesia) we have executive leaders as Apostles, Prophets, Evangelists, Pastors, and Teachers.

These leaders receive instructions from headquarters, where the Lord Jesus Christ is seated at the right hand of the throne of God in Heaven via the Holy Spirit. These executive leaders then impart revelation knowledge received from Heaven to the citizens of the Kingdom of Heaven by preaching and teaching via the Holy Spirit.

Also, individuals can receive confirmation of what they have received because individuals can receive from headquarters just like the executive leaders can via the person of the Holy Spirit. This impartation and confirmation helps us to be effective citizens of the Kingdom of God.

As members of the body of Christ and citizens of the Kingdom of God when we come together for Kingdom business, the purpose is threefold:

- To bestow upon our God, our King, and Holy Spirit the praise and worship that the Godhead is so worthy to receive, thus creating an atmosphere.

- To receive specific instructions about Kingdom operations for this embassy to carry out.

- As ambassadors of the Kingdom of God we to receive instructions and directions, then we are to examine the constitution to see if what we have received is in line with the Word of God. As citizens we are too disseminated to each of our jurisdiction (place of influence) executing these instructions and directions as examples consequently being effective kingdom citizens through our living a Kingdom of God life.

This is similar to the government of the United States. We have elected officials that come from each state to a central location (Washington, DC) to conduct government business making laws on the behalf of the citizens. Then the elected officials will go back to his/her district, state, or jurisdiction that they represent and inform them of the laws, etc.

Summary

Jesus has returned to Heaven after completing his responsibility of restoring the Kingdom of God back on earth. In doing so, He raised up disciples and apostles to continue the preaching of the Gospel of the Kingdom of God\Government of God. He sits on the throne of heaven directing that work through His representatives' (legislative body). Regrettably, most of us do not really understand what Jesus meant when He spoke of the Kingdom. We need to do what Paul said to Timothy in *2 Timothy 2:15,* "Study Jesus' message so that we can accurately articulate and help fulfill His assignment in preparation for His coming back to reign on earth."

As members of the body of Christ, we are the hands, feet, arms, and fingers of God in the earth today. We have been commissioned to continue what He has started. Jesus has returned to Heaven after completing his responsibility of restoring the Kingdom of God back on earth. As representatives of Christ, we should be concerned only with the interests of our King.

Everything we say and do should reflect that desire and that purpose. Our opinions do not matter.

It is completely improper for ambassadors to express their opinions while acting in an official capacity as the representation and voice of their government.

- Jesus *announced* the arrival of the Kingdom of Heaven (*Matthew 4:17*).
- Jesus preached and taught about the Kingdom of God, and its *location* (*Luke 17:21*) for three years prior to His death, burial, and resurrection.

- Jesus taught about the *person of the Holy Spirit* and what He would do when He came after Jesus departed from the earth *(John 14:16-17, 26)*.
- Jesus taught about the *Kingdom of God* for 40 days prior to his ascension to Heaven *(Acts 1-8)*.

A careful study of the biblical message and the presentation of the message of the Kingdom of Heaven by Jesus will illustrate the presence of all these components and characteristics of life in the Kingdom of God. The most outstanding element distinguishing the Kingdom of God from every other kingdom is the concept that all of its citizens are relatives of the king and are kings themselves. This was the message brought to the earth by the Lord Jesus Christ.

Chapter 8
The Kingdom Law of Authority

We have the natural realm that is governed by laws and principles and there is also the realm of the spirit. The natural realm governs by the law of gravity, the laws of electricity, and the laws of aerodynamics. These laws control functions in the natural and the physical realm. In the same way there are laws which govern operations in the realm of the spirit.

> ***Romans 13:1-5 says ...*** *"Let every soul be subject unto the higher powers. For there is no power but of God: the powers that be are ordained of God. ² Whosoever therefore resisteth the power, resisteth the ordinance of God: and they that resist shall receive to themselves damnation. ³ For rulers are not a terror to good works, but to the evil. Wilt thou then not be afraid of the power? do that which is good, and thou shalt have praise of the same: ⁴ For he is the minister of God to thee for good. But if thou do that which is evil, be afraid; for he beareth not the sword in vain: for he is the minister of God, a revenger to execute wrath upon him that doeth evil. ⁵ Wherefore ye must needs be subject, not only for wrath, but also for conscience sake.*

Let us look briefly at an important spiritual law, which governs the operation of all beings in the realm of the spirit. This is necessary for grasping the principle of spiritual jurisdiction. This law is called the law of authority.

> ***Romans 3:27*** "*declares that there is a law of faith.*" This law of faith governs the use of power in the spirit world.

Love is called the "royal law" in *James 2:8*. In *Romans 8:2*, we are introduced to the "law of the Spirit of Life in Christ Jesus" which supersedes the law of sin and death. These are just a few of the laws which govern the realm of the spirit. Just as failure to recognize and adhere to the natural laws God has designed will always prove to be physically disastrous, so will failure to recognize and adhere to the spiritual laws, which God has ordained, will prove to be spiritually disastrous.

> ***Romans 13:1-5 says*** ... "*Let every soul be subject unto the higher powers. For there is no power but of God: the powers that be are ordained of God. ² Whosoever therefore resisteth the power, resisteth the ordinance of God: and they that resist shall receive to themselves damnation. ³ For rulers are not a terror to good works, but to the evil.*

> *Wilt thou then not be afraid of the power? do that which is good, and thou shalt have praise of the same:*
>
> *⁴ For he is the minister of God to thee for good. But if thou do that which is evil, be afraid; for he beareth not the sword in vain: for he is the minister of God, a revenger to execute wrath upon him that doeth evil. ⁵ Wherefore ye must needs be subject, not only for wrath, but also for conscience sake.*

We read in *Romans 13:1-5,* in verses one and two, the word "power" is used several times. This English word "power" is translated from the Greek word "exousia."

The word "exousia", however, should be translated "authority." Although authority and power work together like a hand and glove, they must be recognized as distinctly in the realm of spiritual things.

Let us replace the word "power" with "authority" and take a more accurate look at **Romans 13:1-2:**

> *"Let every soul be subject unto the higher (authorities). For there is no (authority) but of God; the (authorities) that be are ordained of God. Whosoever therefore resisteth the authority resisteth the ordinance of God; and they that resist shall receive to themselves damnation."*

Romans 13:1-2 teaches about a crucial law, which not only governs operations in the natural realm, but also governs operations in the realm of the spirit.

This law is the law of authority. There is a spiritual law that is ordained by God called the law of authority.

God ordained the law of authority. He instituted it and every spiritual being, including ourselves, must cooperate with it. This law controls the operation of every spirit being and must be recognized and adhered to.

This law of authority is one of the greatest keys to understanding and operating in the realm of the spirit. Those who have trouble submitting to the law of authority will have a very difficult time being used of God. In recognizing the law of authority we can begin to understand the significance of the principle of spiritual jurisdiction.

1) What is Spiritual Jurisdiction?

Jurisdiction can be defined as "a range of authority." Range means "scope, boundaries, limitations, or distance."

Authority means "the right to command, enforce, or intervene in a matter." Jurisdiction then means the right to exercise authority within a specific region or territory.

A specific jurisdiction is the range, scope, boundaries or region in which one has the right to command, enforce, or intervene in a matter. Now let us expand our definition of jurisdiction to include the realm of the spirit.

Spiritual jurisdiction is "the boundaries within which a spiritual being has the right to command, enforce, intervene, or exercise power in the realm of the spirit."

All spirit beings have a range or region within which they do have the right to exercise and enforce power. Conversely, all spirit beings have boundaries outside which they do not have the right to exercise or enforce power. This is the law of spiritual jurisdiction.

God has a spiritual jurisdiction. Angels have a certain spiritual jurisdiction. Men, both saved and unsaved, have a spiritual jurisdiction. Satan and his demonic cohorts have a certain spiritual jurisdiction.

The boundary lines of a specific spiritual jurisdiction may be geographic as with cities, states, or even nations but mainly these boundaries pertain to established laws in spiritual matters and spiritual offices.

Spiritual jurisdiction is the law of authority that governs the operation of all beings in the realm of the spirit.

Recognizing the principle of spiritual jurisdiction is vital in all things pertaining to the believer's life. It has implications concerning our relationship with God, our warfare with the enemy, our authority as believers, and our various calls to ministry. In order to understand your place in spiritual matters and operate in your authority you must understand this principle of spiritual jurisdiction.

Having established the basic definition of spiritual jurisdiction, let us focus on how this principle really works.

2) Three Authorities in One World

We must understand that there are three spiritual authorities that have rights to operate. These three authorities are God, Satan, and man.

Some picture the spirit realm as a crazy, haphazard, and unorganized world where it is impossible to predict what is going to happen. However, that is not true. You see, no kingdom, no system, and no realm can function without levels of authority.

There is a law of authority, of rank and order, in the spirit realm. Every being in the spirit realm must operate within the restraints of its boundaries of authority.

The realm of the spirit is a highly organized and structured world and is governed by the law of spiritual jurisdiction. There are boundaries and borders that measure out the extent and limitations of authority of every being in the realm of the spirit, just as the natural realm has boundaries defining the range of police jurisdiction. God has outlined for Himself that He will not transgress!

So there are boundaries in the spirit realm that outline the range of authority of Satan, of demons and angels, of the believer, of ministerial offices, and of anointings. In the Godhead there is rank and authority. Jesus submits to the Father and the Holy Spirit is submitted to the Father and the Son. *(See 1 Corinthians 11:3)*

God's angels have rank and order. *Daniel 10* speaks of chief angels and the higher angels. Michael and Gabriel are examples of such higher angels.

In God's kingdom, there are cherubim, seraphim, and a variety of different angels with different duties and assignments and different levels of authority. None of them step outside their level of authority or their rank.

The kingdom of darkness is also governed by a highly organized and structured system of rank and order (see *Ephesians 6:11-13*).

The law of authority governs the activities of his demonic forces. If you are a student of the Bible, you will have already learned that there are rank and order in the Body of Christ. In order to bless God, we need to act like the army that God is calling us to be. We need to endure hardness, follow orders, submit to those over us in the Lord, and quit breaking rank!

Spiritual jurisdiction has these three authorities: God, Satan, and man (represented by the believer).

A believer must recognize that there are extents and limitations to God's authority, to Satan's authority, and to the authority which man has as a believer.

There was a jurisdiction within which God was able to bless me and outside of which He was not. There is a jurisdiction within which the demons had authority to harass and outside of which they could not.

Man also has a jurisdiction, which is represented by my right to choose which authority man would submit to. There were limitations and boundaries concerning all three of these authorities.

Failure to recognize that God, Satan, and man all have established boundaries within which they have a right to operate and outside of which they do not will keep us from understanding why things happen as they do. We will not know why certain things happen to believers.

Summary

We will not know who is exercising authority and, therefore, will not know who to resist or when to resist. We will not be able to recognize if God is doing something or if it is the devil. We will not understand when to take spiritual initiative and when to rest in faith.

We will not recognize that there are limitations even to God's ability to bless us. We will not understand why our legal authority in Christ seems, at times, to be short-circuited and why Satan seems to be free to exercise his power. We must recognize the extent and limitations of the boundaries of God's authority. We need to know that outside certain boundaries He cannot bless us. We must also realize that within certain boundaries He can and will bless us. We must realize that Satan has certain boundaries within which he can exercise authority. Within certain boundaries, he has authority to harass and torment.

As we learned earlier, we will discover from God's Word that we can step out and stay outside of Satan's boundaries where he and his demons must desist their maneuvers in our lives.

Recognizing and operating within these laws of authority is one of the greatest keys to operating effectively in the realm of the spirit.

Chapter 9
The Kingdom of God citizens dress requirement while on earth

One of the greatest lies Satan seeks to blind Christians to is that "they have no spiritual battle." When Christians do not believe they are in a battle, they will not use their spiritual weapons to fight the devil. This is exactly Why does all he can to try to keep Christians blind to his influence over them.

God wants you and me to recognize an attack. Then we learn how to stay one-step ahead of Satan's attacks against us as much as possible. When he attacks (not if he attacks), we will have the wisdom to know it is a demonic attack. We will purpose to walk ever closer to the Lord in trusting Him to reveal to us how to cooperate with the Lord to demonstrate Satan's defeat.

> *Ephesians 6:13,* "Wherefore take unto you the whole armor of God, that ye may be able to withstand in the evil day, and having done all, to stand"

Kingdom citizen Dressed while on earth

1. The Belt of Truth

> ***Ephesians 6:14,*** *"¹⁴ Stand therefore, **having your loins girt about with truth,** and having on the breastplate of righteousness;"*

The belt that girds it all securely together and demonstrates the believer's readiness for war is truth. Alethia, translated "truth," basically refers to the content of that which is true. One aspect of truth is the content of God's Word, which is absolutely essential for the believer in his battle against the schemes of satan.

Without the truth of Scripture, as the apostle has already pointed out, we are subject to being "carried about by every wind of doctrine, by the trickery of men, by craftiness in deceitful scheming." **(See *Ephesians 4:14*)**

> ***1 Peter 5:8*** *- "Be of sober spirit, be on the alert. Your adversary, the devil, prowls around like a roaring lion, seeking someone to devour".*
>
> ***James 4:7*** *– ""Submit therefore to God. Resist the devil and he will flee from you".*
>
> ***John 8:32*** *– "Ye shall know the truth"*

> ***Hosea 4:6*** *– "My people are destroyed for lack of knowledge: because thou hast rejected knowledge, I will also reject thee, that thou shalt be no priest to me: seeing thou hast forgotten the law of thy God, I will also forget thy children"*

The belt that girds it all securely together and demonstrates the believer's readiness for war is truth. Alethia, translated "truth," basically refers to the content of that which is true. One aspect of truth is the content of God's Word, which is absolutely essential for the believer in his battle against the schemes of satan.

2. The Breast Plate of Righteousness

> ***Ephesians 6:14*** *– "Stand firm therefore, having girded your loins with truth, and having put on **the breastplate of righteousness**"*

The purpose of that piece of armor is obvious — to protect the heart, lungs, intestines, and other vital organs. The breastplate of righteousness that we put on is part spiritual armor against our adversary. This is the practical righteousness of a life lived in obedience to God's Word.

It is righteous behavior of the believer as found in *Ephesians 4:24-27,* which having been done, will "not give the devil opportunity" (*Colossians 3:9-14. 1 Corinthians 1:30,* and *2 Corinthians 5:21).*

The breastplate is then put on to protect men and help believers in righteousness and along with the belt. This armor is never to be removed.

No Roman soldier would go into battle without his breastplate--a tough, sleeveless piece of armor that covered his full torso. It was often made of leather or heavy linen, onto which were sewn overlapping slices of animal hooves, horns, or pieces of metal. Some were made of large pieces of metal molded or hammered to conform to the body.

3. The Shoes of the Gospel of Peace

> ***Ephesians 6:15*** *– "And having **shod your feet** with the preparation of the gospel of peace…"*

The purpose of shoes (boots) allows the soldier to be ready to march, climb, fight, or do whatever else is necessary. It is not a fashion statement.

Roman soldiers' shoes had a much different purpose than the shoes you may have on because a soldier's very life could depend on them.

As he marches on rough hot roads, climbs over jagged rocks, tramples over thorns, and wades through streambeds of jagged stones, his feet would need much protection. A soldier whose feet is blistered, cut, or swollen cannot fight well and often is not even able to stand up to the perilous situations in battle.

A Christian's spiritual footwear is equally important. Verse 15 says, "And your feet shod with the preparation of the gospel of peace." The Greek word for preparation has the general meaning of readiness.

4. The Shield of Faith

> *Ephesians 6:16 -* "*In addition to all, taking up **the shield of faith** with which you will be able to extinguish all the flaming arrows of the evil one*".
>
> *1 John 5:4 –* "*For whatever is born of God overcomes the world; and this is the victory that has overcome the world our faith*"

Every word of God is tested, He is a shield to those who take refuge in Him. Do not add to His words or He will reprove you, and you will be proved a liar." *(Proverbs 30:5-6)*

A shield can be a very threatening thing. I cannot think of a shield that has flowers on it or a happy face. Most shields have emblems on them that invoke fear. An army that is advancing wants to strike fear in the hearts of their enemy. Fear can be very damaging.

Paul explains the need to be equipped with the shield of faith. He has a break here in the list of armor. "In addition to all" introduces the last three pieces of armor.

The first three--the belt, breastplate, and shoes were for long-range preparation and protection and were never taken off on the battlefield. The shield, helmet, and sword, on the other hand, were kept in readiness for use when actual fighting began.

The soldiers who carried these shields were in the front lines of battle and normally stood side by side with their shields together, forming a horizontal wall extending as long as a mile or more.

- This kind of a stance would strike fear in the enemy because from a distance it was hard to see where the break was. It looked like a solid wall.

- The shields were also useful in the aerial attack.

- The archers stood behind this protective wall of shields and shot their arrows as they advanced against the enemy. Anyone who stood or crouched behind such shields was protected from the barrage of enemy arrows and spears.

The shield, which had a covering of metal or leather soaked in water, was the most reliable protection against such flaming missiles because it would either deflect or extinguish them. The devil continually bombards God's children with temptations to immorality, hatred, envy, anger, covetousness, pride, doubt, fear, despair, distrust, and every other sin. These sound like fiery missiles to me.

satan's initial temptation to Adam and Eve was to entice them to doubt God and instead to put their trust in his lies. The first of his flaming missiles, from which all the others have lighted their flames, every temptation, directly or indirectly, is the temptation to doubt and distrust God.

5. The Helmet of Salvation

> ***Ephesians 6:17*** *- "And take **the helmet of salvation**, and the sword of the Spirit, which is the word of God"*

> ***1 Thessalonians 5:8*** *- "But since we are of the day, let us be sober, having put on the breastplate of faith and love, and as a helmet, the hope of salvation"*

The purpose of the helmet of salvation is to prevent head injuries because head injuries are a serious issue.

There have been accidents where victims had what seemed to be minor injuries, but because there was a blow to the head, they had serious head trauma. Even people riding bicycles can have serious head injuries if they fall.

Think about it. Would you want to play professional football with no helmet? That is why we need this protection.

satan has a double-edged sword, which he attacks the believer with discouragement when he points to our failures, our sins, and our unresolved problems. Doubt is design to separate us from truly knowing and following Christ wholeheartedly.

Doubt is the very reason why a person has trouble-knowing God more through prayer and scripture. We may be tempted to doubt our calling, our choice in a marriage partner, our job, our abilities, and so many other things. Doubt has a tendency to cripple us just as a head injury may cripple someone who otherwise is perfectly healthy.

6. Sword of the Spirit

> ***Ephesians 6:17*** *- "And take the helmet of salvation, and **the sword of the Spirit**, which is the word of God"*

> ***Hebrews 4:12*** *- "For the word of God is living and active and sharper than any two-edged sword, and piercing as far as the division of soul and spirit, of both joints and marrow, and able to judge the thoughts and intentions of the heart"*

The other parts of his armor are meant to withstand the attacks of the enemy, but the weapon he carries is meant to attack, to strew down those that stand before him.

I am sure a shield can become a weapon, but not nearly as effectively as a sword or gun. A weapon can shout death and defeat to those who come against it. It brings this sense of fear because the bigger the weapon the greater the fall.

Why it is then that believers should put on the entire armor, except for their swords? Those that do pick up the sword are not sure how to use it or may even cut themselves before they are a threat to the enemy.

Paul says that our weapon is the sword of the Spirit, which is the Word of God. This type of sword was able to be pulled out quickly and thrust into the enemy when under attack.

The more familiar we are with the weapon, the better equipped we are to use it correctly and the better equipped we are in keeping it in good working condition and keeping ourselves safe.

The Holy Spirit is our helper or trainer and will teach us and help us to remember what we have been taught.

There are others that can help us in this training as well, although the Holy Spirit is our top trainer. We can call upon friends, pastors, and family members to help us in this training.

How to practice the use of Scripture:
(1) Read God's Word
(2) Know God's Word
(3) Meditate on God's Word
(4) Hide God's Word in your heart

When we pick up the sword of the Spirit, we become an offensive soldier. We will be able to expose deeds of darkness through the Word of God. The word is a light, which will shine out in the darkness and expose all that is in it. *(See Ephesians 5:13; Psalm 119:105, 130).*

We can refute worldly philosophies and false religions. God's Word is truth and will refute the false claims and the misguided *(James 5:19-20).* Preach the Gospel of Salvation; the greatest way that we can damage the kingdom of Satan is to turn people away from satan to Christ Jesus through the Gospel.

2 Timothy 3:16-17 *- "All scripture is inspired by God and profitable for teaching, for reproof, for correction, for training in righteousness, so that the man of God may be adequate, equipped for every good work."*

7. Praying through the Armor of God with all Prayers

Ephesians 6:13 *- "Therefore, take up the full armor of God, so that you will be able to resist in the evil day, and having done everything, to stand firm"*

We are to put on the armor of God. It is only then that we will be able to stand up against the onslaught that Satan has for us each day. I do not think there is one of us who would want to be plopped down in the middle of a battlefield with no armor.

The devil will come against us in a multitude of ways:

- **Undermining** - God's character and credibility
- **Persecution** - peer pressure or peaceful preoccupation
- **Confusing** - the believer with false doctrine
- **Hindering** - the believer's service to Christ
- **Causing** - division in the Body of Christ
- **Urging** - believers to trust their own resources
- **Causing** - the believer to be hypercritical
- **Making** - believers worldly and causing us to disobey God's Word.

Although it is very important to be aware of the devices of Satan, our defense against them is not simply our knowledge of them.

The armor has been provided for daily battle we are in. We can be equipped with this armor through the power of prayer.

PRAY IN THE SPIRIT, and intercede for all Christians as the Holy Spirit prompts me. I believe that the Holy Spirit is interceding on my behalf, according to my prayers.

> *Jude 20 - "But ye, beloved, building up yourselves on your most holy faith, praying in the Holy Ghost."*
>
> *James 5:14-16, - "Is any sick among you? Let him call for the elders of the church; and let them pray over him, anointing him with oil in the name of the Lord: 15And the prayer of faith shall save the sick, and the Lord shall raise him up; and if he have committed sins, they shall be forgiven him. 16Confess your faults one to another, and pray one for another, that ye may be healed."*

The effectual fervent prayer of a righteous man availeth much.

> ***Romans 8:26-28,*** *- "Likewise the Spirit also helpeth our infirmities; for we know not what we should pray for as we ought; but the Spirit itself maketh intercession for us with groanings which cannot be uttered. ²⁷And he that searcheth the hearts knoweth what is the mind of the Spirit, because he maketh intercession for the saints according to the will of God. ²⁸And we know that all things work together for good to them that love God, to them who are the called according to his purpose.*

Heavenly Father, I come afresh today ___/___/___. I submit my spirit, soul, mind, will, emotions, imagination, and present my body and my sensory mechanism to YOUR HAND. I lay my life on the altar of consecration before YOU. Heavenly Father, I come thanking you for your word and for the leading of the Holy Spirit, desiring that you will be down in my life.

I want to be like my Lord and Savior who lived a life in daily intimacy of closeness and in constant fellowship with you. Heavenly Father, I want to know your will more clearly, with absolute certainty of divine guidance with instructions on not only what to do, but how to do it.

Heavenly Father, work in me to do YOUR will and to do YOUR good pleasure because for that purpose I am here in the earth only to do your will. Heavenly Father, you are Almighty God "El-Elyon," the Most High, I bless and praise you in Jesus name, Amen.

Summary
Spiritually Dressed For Success

When we put on the Armor of God, we are putting on the Lord Jesus Christ, can you see the wonderful provision of God that we have in Christ. For instance, **Number 1***, we have the belt of truth. Jesus said He is the truth (See John 14:6).* **Number 2***, we have the breastplate of righteousness, and the Bible says that Jesus has been made unto us <u>our righteousness</u> (See 1 Corinthians 1:30).* **Number 3***, we are to wear the shoes of the gospel of peace, and we read that Jesus Himself is <u>our peace</u> (See Ephesians 2:14).* **Number 4***, we have the shield of faith, and the Bible says that Jesus is the author and the perfect of our faith (See Hebrews 12:2).* **Number 5***, we have the helmet of salvation, and Jesus' title is Savior (See John 1:1).* **Number 6***, we have the sword of the spirit, the word of God (See Hebrews 12:2).* **Number 7***, we get Dress to Pray*

Chapter 10
The Kingdom of God Operation of Faith

It is through faith that we activate and access the things that our loving Heavenly Father has provided for us to enjoy in the here and now!

Faith is the currency of the Kingdom, if you want anything in the kingdom it must be access by faith

Faith is acting on the WORD. It is not on your sensory mechanism, some philosophical reasoning, nor on theological concepts, but it's acting on God's Word.

> *Romans 10:9-10 (NTL) says...* "If you confess with your mouth that Jesus is Lord and believe in your heart that God raised him from the dead, you will be saved For it is by believing in your heart that you are made right with God, and it is by confessing with your mouth that you are saved."
>
> *Romans 3:27* we find, "27Where is boasting then? It is excluded. By what law? of works? Nay: but by the law of faith."

In order to participate in the operation of faith you must have *three* things:

1. You must have the Word of God *(Logos\Rhema)*
2. A Heart that believes the Word of God *(1 Peter 3:4)*
3. A Mouth that speaks (confesses) the Word of God *(Proverb 18:21)*

Some scriptural illustrations are given to show what the Word of God is teaching us - the secret of faith. To be a co-labor with the Spirit of God, it is necessary to know what the ground rules are so that we can operate in faith.

Listed below some examples of the Operations of Faith:

1. God said, "Let there be, Let Them, and Let us" *Genesis 1:3-26,* "Father of many nations" *Genesis 17:3-5*
2. Conquest of Jericho: *Joshua 6:1-16, 20;* "Walk around the wall"
3. Naaman, the Syria healed: *2 King 5:1-4, 8 -14;* "Dip seven times"
4. Peter acting on the Word of God: *Luke 5:1-9; (v5)* "let down the net"

The simplest way to the operation of faith, is learn to believe the Word to the point that you will act on it. You don't know if you are really a believer until you are willing to demonstrate your belief.

It is through acting on the Word of God that you move from believing to faith. *James 1:22* states that, "We are not to be hearers only, but doers of the Word of God."

The operation of faith calls those things, which be not as though they were. Instead of them being based upon what you see; they are based upon the Word of God.

The universe, in which live, contain many laws. One that we are very familiar with is the law of gravity. Everyone knows what goes up must come down.

The law, by which we access the things of God, is called the Law of Faith.

The Law of Faith, operates when we learn to, "Call those things which be not as though they were", according to 2 *Corinthians 4:18*. We can apply this law, because we are born-again.

There are many who operate in faith from a negative prospective. Listed below are some examples of negative phrases that people use without realizing it.

1. "My feet are killing me." (1 Peter 2:24)
2. "I am scared to death." (2 Timothy 1:7)
3. "I am confused." (1 Corinthians 14:30)
4. "I am broke, busted, and can't be trusted" (Phil. 4:19)
5. "Well if it's not one things it is another" (Mark 11:23)
6. "I am so weak" (Joel 3:10b)
7. "Girl I am about to lose my mind" (1Corinthians 2:16)

We, as believers, have the ability of operate in faith without an understanding the workings of faith. It is the enemy who is influencing us to use such phrases because he knows that it is detrimental to our lives. By understanding the proper working of faith, we can receive the wonderful blessings of God.

> Romans 5:1-3 "Therefore being justified by faith, we have peace with God through Our Lord Jesus Christ: By whom also we have access by faith into this grace wherein we stand, and rejoice in hope of the glory of God and not only so, but we glory in tribulations also: knowing that tribulation worketh patience;"

As believers, we have the God kind of faith and must act according to

> Mark 11:22-24; "And Jesus answering saith unto them, have faith in God. ²³For verily I say unto you, That whosoever shall say unto this mountain, Be thou removed, and be thou cast into the sea; and shall not doubt in his heart, but shall believe that those things which he saith shall come to pass; he shall have whatsoever he saith. ²⁴Therefore I say unto you, what things soever ye desire, when ye pray, believe that ye receive them, and ye shall have them."

I trust that you have seen from the biblical examples how the operations of the God kind of faith, works. In order to be successful in the things of God, it is necessary to know what the ground rules are, so that we can be co-laborers with the Spirit of God. It is through faith that we have access to the wonderful blessings that He has for us to enjoy while on earth.

Summary

Faith is trusting in God and not man. For man has the ability to fail, whereas, God never fails. When you walk by faith, there is no room for doubts. When you walk by faith, there is no time for worries. When you walk by faith, mountains will be moved. Always know God's word, have a believing heart and confess with your mouth God's word. According to Hebrews 11:6, it states that without faith it is impossible to please God,

Chapter 11
Kingdom of God citizens steps to citizens Maturity

One of the great concerns of new parents is the normal and healthy growth of their newborn. Doctors know precisely how much weight should be gained, and if the child does not follow this pattern, the doctor seeks to determine the problem, if any. Parents are greatly concerned with the maturity of their children. The same is true with our Heavenly Father, who is concerned with the maturity of His children and expects each of His children to grow so that we may reach the level of maturity of full grown, active citizens in His kingdom.

Spiritual Maturity is a process

It is a process, which begins when a person accepts Jesus Christ as their Lord and Savior. He or she is born again. The objective of spiritual maturity is to recognize that you are a spirit, you have a soul, and you live in a physical body.

Spiritual maturity is the process of allowing our spirit to take his rightful place as king, our soul as servant, and our body as the slave.

We are to recognize that the Holy Spirit is within our spirits.

> **1 John 4:4;** *"Greater is He that in you than He that is in the world." The Old Testament offers an illustration to help us better understand this idea.*

In the [Book(s) of the Bible], we see Moses/Solomon Whoever building the Tabernacle, (define what the Tabernacle was or why it was built, e.g. a place built for the purpose of worshiping God.)

The Tabernacle was constructed with three levels: the outer court, inner court, and the Holy of Holies (what is the significance of each level? This way the next sentence makes more sense).

Our bodies are outer court, our souls are the inner court, and our spirits are the Holy of Holies. Please understand that maturing is a process. Today, society promotes instant gratification, whereby everybody wants what they want, when they want it – which is typically immediately.

This culture frequently forgets the important and necessary role of process. Consider restoration of damaged drywall.

Not long ago I had a small kitchen fire, and in the process of putting out the fire, a young overzealous fireman damaged a wall leading to the kitchen.

I hired a contractor to restore the damage, and he informed me that the repair would be a process:

- The <u>First Step</u> is to cut out the damaged area of the drywall.

- The <u>Second Step</u> is to replace the damaged drywall with new drywall by sealing it with drywall nails, tape, and compound (drywall repair kit).

- The <u>Third Step</u>, after the compound dries, which takes several hours, the area must be sanded down. If needed, more compound is applied, followed by more sanding to get the area as smooth as possible.

- The <u>Fourth Step</u> involves adding the first coat of paint, or primer, which will need time to dry. Finally, add the finishing coat of paint and wait for it to dry.

- This <u>PROCESS may take several days</u>. It is not instant or immediate. Similarly, maturing is neither instant or immediately. It is a process, but you as an individual can determine the length of time it takes by being diligent and operating in excellence.

Our loving Heavenly Father, to ensure that His children grow, has placed within His Holy Word a maturity plan.

As Christians, our spiritual maturity level should be to the point that we instantly obey the Spirit of God (Holy Spirit within our spirit) without any interference from our soul (mind/will/emotion) or the body (feelings\flesh and the sensor mechanism.)

A life that is submitted to the Lord and to the leadership of the Holy Spirit will be a life that is vastly different from that which is submitted to the corruption of this world.

Three Levels or stages of Spiritual Development

Spiritual Development is the process of our becoming more like Jesus Christ and bringing God greater glory. These levels or stages correspond to the childhood, youth or teenage years, and adulthood of physical life.

1. The Stage of Spiritual Childhood

Baby Christians are those who just or recently experience receiving Jesus as personal and Lord.

People at this stage of spiritual growth are still coming to grips with the exciting fact that Jesus Christ has forgiven all their sins and they have been rescued from judgment and eternal death.

Baby Christians are dependent on others. They need someone to feed them and help them make their way along in the spiritual life.

A baby or young child cannot function on its own. Baby Christians do not know how to live life yet because they have not been alive in Christ long enough to know how to live.

2. Becoming a Spiritual Young Person

This stage, becoming a spiritual young person or youth, which can reach from the teenage years into the early years of what the world considers young adulthood.

This period of life is marked by conflict and the need to become spiritually strong and learn how to overcome the devil.

At this stage, a young person is coming to grips with the realities of the Christian life and is often engaged in real combat with the devil.

These are the years of the Christian life when we first learn how to use the sword of the Spirit, God's Word, to counter the attacks of the Enemy.

3. Becoming a Mature Adult

The mature believer knows God in a depth of intimacy that has been developing over time. A mature Christian has come to know God over time through the growth process and the scars obtained in spiritual battle through demonstrating the devil defeat. There are still battles with the Enemy to fight and his defeat must be demonstrated.

Mature Christian's life has a quality of depth about it that can only be gained by going through the process of applying the WORD of God.

How do you know when you know God in such an intimate way? The short answer is that your spirit is able to commune with God at such a deep level that you pick up leading of the Holy Spirit that other folk miss.

In 2 Peter 1:5-7, Peter uses an illustration of a staircase that leads from one level to another.

Peter lists eight steps of a life that is submitted to the Lord. If one claims the faith, but does not find these virtues to be growing in their lives, their claim becomes questionable.

Peter exhorts his readers to make their calling certain, by faith and other virtues

> **2 Peter 1:5-7,** *"And beside this, giving all diligence, add to your faith virtue; and to virtue knowledge;⁶ And to knowledge temperance; and to temperance patience; and to patience godliness; ⁷ And to godliness brotherly kindness; and to brotherly kindness charity.*

These steps represent the development of relationships, moving from one level to another. Again, this is an ongoing process as we take the necessary steps toward spiritual maturity.

If one continually apply each of these eight steps listed below, integrating them more and more into daily life, the result is a life that is transformed from the corrupt nature of this world to the very nature of God. Along with these steps, there are two key words that I want to reiterate: diligence and excellence. These two words must be understood and applied if we want to mature as a child of God. (*See 2 Peter 1:1-10;*)

The Bible says grace and peace be multiplied unto you through the knowledge of God and that God has given everything that pertains unto life and godliness, through the knowledge of Him (diligence).

Let us now look to define some of the key concepts in this passage:

1. **Faith** gets us into God's family, and forms the foundation which our life should rest upon.

2. **Virtue** keeps us from getting trapped and defeated by sin. As a Christian, our virtues (morals) are established by the Bible.

3. **Knowledge** gives us the answers for the problems we go through and for the uncertainties in times of troubles.

4. **Temperance** helps us control ourselves when we want to do wrong.

5. **Patience** enables us to wait on God and grow at the same time. No matter what we are confronted with, God's grace is sufficient enough to get us through.

6. **Godliness** is what happens when we surrender our Will desires, to God, and we live a life that pleases him. We end up looking more like him.

7. **Brotherly Kindness** is loving to treat other believers like family.

8. **Charity** (Agape) is God's love, which is not based on performance or feelings. It is a simple decision based upon the love of God that has shed abroad in our heart, which is directed towards everyone, the rarest form of love.

Chapter 12
Manifestation of the Kingdom of God Sons/Daughters

We have shared about the understanding of the Kingdom of God Government. It is one thing to read about the government of God, but it is another thing to apply what you have just read. In this chapter I want to share about the *manifestation of the Sons of God*; this is an end time message. **(see *Romans 8:14-23*)**

We are preparing for the return of Jesus Christ. There is some serious work that needs to be done as the church ages to a close and the millennium reign of Christ. I believe that we are about to witness the greatest move of God that the world has ever experienced. I believe that we are going to be a part of it. I believe there has to be a maturing of Christians.

The church is the called out one (Greek word ecclesia). This has the idea of the State of the Union, which meets in February each year.

When they meet, you have the elected official that comes from each state. They go to a place that make laws--to do some other governmental business at one central location, and to have a meeting on the behalf of the people.

Then these elected officials go back to their district or state that they represent. As we see at the church, this is what we are to be like. This is not a religious meeting but a time of praise and worshipping, receiving instruction and knowledge for living the Christian life or to become a better kingdom citizen.

We the church are the called out ones and we the church are the most powerful, intuitive organism on planet earth. While we are meeting, the executive members (apostle, prophet, evangelist, pastor, or teacher) may be speaking, but the Holy Spirit may be speaking to you at the same time.

When we come to church, we are experiencing something similar to the state of the Union message, are truly having a Kingdom of God meeting.

We are downloading from God because according to

> *Revelation 17:14*, "for he is Lord of lords, and King of kings:"

> *Matthew 16:18*, "Upon this rock I will build my church; the **gates** of **hell** shall not prevail against it."

The kingdom of darkness cannot stop the forward progress of the Church. We are broadcast out into the world or our designated area and take rulership, influence, and impact that area for the Kingdom of God.

God expects us to take over the area where we have been sent, and bring it under or in subjection to the Kingdom of God--Thy kingdom come, Thy will be done on earth as in heaven. Anything that is out of line we are to bring it in line.

We can see that things are out of line. It is the Babylon systems that Satan and his demonic spirit has set up. We have the ability and authority to bring our areas of responsibility back in line with the Kingdom of God. When the apostles hear the church they did not hear religion but they heard a ruling body.

We have been CALLED out by Almighty God. We are the ambassadors of God. We have diplomatic functions wherein we are passing through the earth doing kingdom business (*2 Corinthians 5:17-21*).

We all come into this world as a baby and the same is true when we come into the body of Christ. Our kinship with God goes off as a baby in Christ.

> ***1 Peter 2:2,*** *"²As newborn babes desire the sincere milk of the word that ye may grow thereby."*

It is important that we make the paradigm right. It is the style that you view yourself as something of value. It is a model that is on our minds, a template and a map of the mind. It is the way that we see things.

> ***Isaiah 55:8-9****, God said…"⁸ For my thoughts are not your thoughts, neither are your ways my ways, saith the* LORD. *⁹ For as the heavens are higher than the earth, so are my ways higher than your ways, and my thoughts than your thoughts.*

Why did God say this? If we are starting to shift our paradigm, we must modify our mental map. If you try to change your behavior without changing your mental map, you are accidentally going somewhere.

Your mindset will overcome your behavior and transport you backward to the way you use to be. You must understand this—it is out of your mental map that your behavior flows.

A man composed a book on how to become a billionaire. If you think like a billionaire, you cannot help but to become a billionaire. It is really just as simple as that. All you have to do is change your thinking.

This not only applies to money but anything--how you deal with your spouse, your friends, and so on.

Take for instance the house that you were raised in, if your parents fought all the time, when you get married you will perform the same thing because that has been normal for you. Simply because it was normal does not make it right however. In order to change your behavior, you must change your map (mental map).

> ***Galatians 4:1-7 says...*** *"Now I say, that the heir, as long as he is a child, differeth nothing from a servant, though he be lord of all; 2 But is under tutors and governors until the time appointed of the father. 3 Even so we, when we were children, were in bondage under the elements of the world: 4 But when the fulness of the time was come,*

> *God sent forth his Son, made of a woman, made under the law, ⁵ To redeem them that were under the law, that we might receive the adoption of sons. ⁶ And because ye are sons, God hath sent forth the Spirit of his Son into your hearts, crying, Abba, Father. ⁷ Wherefore thou art no more a servant, but a son; and if a son, then an heir of God through Christ.*

Once you have realized who you are, you will take on a right identity and then move up to a higher level.

> ***Hebrews 5:12-14** says…* *"¹² For when for the time ye ought to be teachers, ye have need that one teach you again which be the first principles of the oracles of God; and are become such as have need of milk, and not of strong meat. ¹³ For every one that useth milk is unskilful in the word of righteousness: for he is a babe. ¹⁴ But strong meat belongeth to them that are of full age, even those who by reason of use have their senses exercised to discern both good and evil.*

> ***1 Corinthians 3:1-3** says…* *"3 And I, brethren, could not speak unto you as unto spiritual, but as unto carnal, even as unto babes in Christ. ² I have fed you with milk, and not with meat: for hitherto ye were not able to bear it, neither yet now are ye able. ³ For ye are yet carnal: for whereas there is among you envying, and strife, and divisions, are ye not carnal, and walk as men?"*

> ***John 17:14-17** says…* *"¹⁴I have given them thy word; and the world hath hated them, because they are not of the world, even as I am not of the world. ¹⁵I pray not that thou shouldest take them out of the world, but that thou shouldest keep them from the evil. ¹⁶They are not of the world, even as I am not of the world. ¹⁷Sanctify them through thy truth: thy word is truth."*

The only thing that will cause us to grow is the Word of God! That means reading, studying, meditating, and applying or practicing the Word of God.

> ***Ephesians 6:10,*** *"Finally, my brethren, be **strong** in the Lord, and in the power of his might."*

Please know that Satan cannot go beyond his stage of development. Then as we look at this and make it down to a common denominator, the problem is the church has not GROWN up as it should. Our problem is not the devil. The problem is that we have not grown as we should.

We as the church are not supposed to be manipulated by the circumstances or situations and the world systems. We are to be in dominion over all the earth, not some of the earth.

We are sent out into the earth. God expects us to rule the area where we have been sent and bring it under or subject to the Kingdom of God. Thy kingdom come, Thy will be done on earth as in heaven. We can see that things are out of line. It is the Babylon systems that satan has set up.

God has established in His Word the plan or process that is designed to grow us from strength to strength, faith to faith, and glory to glory thus causing the manifestations of his sons.

The devil diabolical plan is to bring humans into bondage through the influence of his demonic forces operating behind the scenes.

Spiritual Maturity is a Process

A process begins when a person accepts Jesus Christ as their Lord and Savior. He or she is born again. The objective of spiritual maturity is to recognize that you are a spirit, you have a soul, and you live in a physical body.

Spiritual maturity is the process of allowing our spirit to take his rightful place as king, our soul as a servant, and our body as the slave. In a previous chapter we explained the makeup of mankind. We are to know that the Holy Spirit is within our spirits according to 1 John 4:4.

> *1 John 4:4 says... "4 Ye are of God, little children, and have overcome them: because greater is he that is in you, than he that is in the world."*

In the [Book(s) of the Bible], we see Moses/Solomon (whoever) building the Tabernacle. Define what the Tabernacle was or why it was built, e.g., a place built for the purpose of worshipping God.

The Tabernacle was constructed with three levels: the outer court, the inner court, and the Holy of Holies. What is the significance of each level?

Our bodies are the outer court, our souls are the inner court, and our spirits are the Holy of Holies. Please understand that maturing is a process. Today, society promotes instant gratification whereby everybody wants what they want, when they want it-- which is typically immediately.

Our loving Heavenly Father, to ensure that His children grow has placed within His Holy Word a maturity program. As Christians, our spiritual maturity level should be to the point that we instantly obey the Spirit of God (Holy Spirit within our spirit) without any interference from our soul (mind/will/emotion) or the body (feelings\flesh and the sensor mechanism).

A spirit that is presented to the Lord and to the leadership of the Holy Spirit will be a life that is immensely dissimilar from that which is submitted to the depravity of this Earth.

Peter lists eight steps of a life that is submitted to the Lord. If one claims the faith but does seek these virtues in order to grow their lives, their claim becomes questionable.

Peter exhorts his readers to make their calling certain, by faith and other virtues.

> ***2 Peter 1:5-7 says...*** *"⁵ And beside this, giving all diligence, add to your faith virtue; and to virtue knowledge; ⁶ And to knowledge temperance; and to temperance patience; and to patience godliness; ⁷ And to godliness brotherly kindness; and to brotherly kindness charity.*

Summary

These steps represent the development of relationships moving from one level to another. Again, this is an ongoing process as we take the necessary steps toward spiritual maturity.

If one continually applies each of these eight steps listed below integrating them more and more into daily life, the result is a spirit that is translated from the tainted nature of this world to the very nature of God. Along with these steps, there are two key words that I want to reiterate: diligence and excellence. These two words must be seen and enforced if we require to grow as a child of God. *(See 2 Peter 1:1-10)*

The Bible says grace and peace be multiplied unto you through the knowledge of God and that God has given everything that pertains unto life and godliness, through the knowledge of Him (diligence).

Let us now look to define some of the central concepts in this transition.

1. **Faith** brings us into God's family and forges the foundation which our life should lie upon.
2. **Virtue** keeps us from becoming trapped and defeated by sin. As a Christian, our virtues (morals) are presented by the Bible.
3. **Knowledge** gives us the responses to the problems we go through and for the uncertainties in times of troubles.
4. **Temperance** helps us control ourselves when we want to do wrong.
5. **Patience** enables us to wait on God and mature at the same time. No matter what we are faced with, God's grace is sufficient enough to take us through.
6. **Godliness** is what happens when we surrender our will desires and to God and we live a life that pleases him. We end up being more like him.

7. **Brotherly kindness** is loving to treat other believers like family.
8. **Charity is God's love** which is not founded on performance or feelings. It is a simple conclusion based upon the passion of God that is shed abroad in our spirit which is directed towards everyone--the rarest kind of lovemaking.

Chapter 13
How to know if you are operating in the Kingdom of God?

How you can know that you are operating in the Kingdom of God? The key to operating in the Kingdom of God is peace. Peace comes to us in two forms both of which will be discussed.

First is the type of peace that we are most familiar with. It is the peace that the world has to offer which is in the natural. It is a state of tranquility or quiet, a freedom from civil disturbance, a state of security or order within a community provided for by law or custom, freedom from disquieting or oppressive thoughts or emotions, and harmony in personal relations.

The world in which we live says that to know peace we must either go somewhere (head to the Bahamas, Hawaii), buy something (a luxury car which shuts out the harshness of the world), or ingest something (get a prescription for a sedative).

The second type of peace is the Hebrew word SHALOM which occurs 236 times within the Holy Scriptures. It takes 20 words in the natural to define the peace of God: completeness, wholeness, health and healing, welfare, safety, salvation, deliverance, soundness, tranquility, prosperity, perfectness, fullness, rest, harmony (unity), absence of agitation or discord, total well-being (all things intact, nothing missing).

In the midst of a stressful life, most people are looking for peace—a state of tranquility—quietness and freedom from confusion!

The peace we crave that Jesus offers is more than that. It is something that only Jesus can give. Jesus tells us that it is HIS peace that He gives to us. He alone has the authority to extend this peace. It is unique to Him.

Three Stages of Peace

A) **Peace with God** - Because of what Jesus had done - *Romans 5:1*, "Therefore being justified by faith, we have peace with God through our Lord Jesus Christ."

B) **The Peace of God** - *Romans 14:17*, "For the Kingdom of God is not meat and drink; but righteousness, and peace, and joy in the Holy Ghost."

- Righteousness, Peace, and Joy

C) **The God of Peace** – This is to be manifested from your life. *Romans 16:20*, "And the God of peace shall bruise Satan under your feet shortly. The grace of our Lord Jesus Christ be with you. Amen."

Who is the source of true peace?

> *John 14:27....* "*27 Peace I leave with you, my peace I give unto you: not as the world giveth, give I unto you. Let not your heart be troubled, neither let it be afraid.*"

This peace is not found in worldly, religious meditation, drugs, and achievements. The peace that we yearn for is something that can only be found in Christ. It may be that the very reason you are searching because they know that you need something for your life. You know there is an emptiness--you know you need something.

How do we get this peace with God?

> *Romans 5:1, "Therefore being justified by faith, we have peace with God through our Lord Jesus Christ:"*

Is it possible to live in continual peace? To the people in the world, that seems like such an impossible goal to reach. Yet the heart of man yearns to experience peace.

Almost continually, we hear accounts in the news about different organizations or governments that are trying to bring peace between conflicting groups and nations. People all over the world want to live in peace, not turmoil.

We can have peace with each other. The peace of God is a peace that restores relationships. All throughout the New Testament we see barriers being lifted between people: Jew, Gentile, black or white, slave, free, male, and female. We all are seeking to glorify Him in our lives. We are not competing with each other we are working with each other. See only through Jesus Christ can we have peace with God and we can have the peace of God. *(See James 3:16)*

His peace keeps our hearts and minds free of confusion and helps us live victoriously. (see *Philippians 4:7-8*)

God's name is peace, Jehovah Shalom, the Lord, my peace and wholeness (*Judges 6:24, Matthew 11:28-29, John 14:27*), the God of peace. "The God of Peace shall bruise the satan under your feet." *(See Romans 16:20)*

The prince of peace is infinitely more powerful and effective than contending and striving in prayer with an anxious and troubled spirit. Peace is power, and a weapon.

Jesus' Routine - Jesus as the head of His body would not require you to do something that He did not do. (See *John 14:12*)

Whether we realize it or not we all have a routine, but we are to follow Jesus' routine because He was a sample son.

Jesus came to show us how a man being led by the Holy Spirit can walk the face of the earth and demonstrate the devil defeat and live in total victory while here on earth. If you examine the four gospels, Jesus never called a person to receive him. Jesus did call for the people to follow Him meaning to do what He did.

The Apostles of Christ did not receive salvation until *John 20:22*, "And when he had said this, he breathed on them, and saith unto them, receive ye the Holy Ghost."

This was after Jesus' resurrection. The apostles did not receive the baptism of the Holy Spirit until the day of Pentecost. In **Romans 10:9-10**, we see that you must receive Jesus as your Lord and Savior. See scripture references **Mark 1:9-12, Matthew 14:23, Mark 1:35-39, Luke 6:12, John 5:19b, John 8:38, and Acts 10:38.**

In the world ye shall have tribulation; but be of good cheer; I have overcome the world. *John 16:33*; But strong meat belongeth to them that are of full age, even those who by reason of use have their senses exercised to discern both good and evil.

The Enemies of Peace

There is no peace now for two reasons: the opposition of Satan and the disobedience of man. The fall of the angels and the fall of man established a world without peace. Satan and man engage with the God of peace in a battle for sovereignty. *(See James 3:16 "giving place to the devil" and 1 Thessalonians 13:33).*

- **Sin Rebellion** - Creates strife and distance between our heavenly Father and us. As a result, we feel the conviction of sin and our peace evaporates.

- **Unbelief** - When we doubt God's promises, uncertainty and fear replace ours. We should have confidence that He will supply all our needs (see *Philippians 4:19*).

- **Mistreatment** - Although criticism from others may threaten our peace, no one can take it unless we give it up. Instead of believing people's unkind or false words, we can choose to hold on to God's peace.

- **Worry** - Anxiety is projecting tomorrow's cares upon today results in worry and anxiety. Jesus said, "Do not worry about tomorrow; for tomorrow will care for itself.

Each day has enough trouble of its own." *(See Matthew 6:34).*

If these were to be banished, we should enjoy infallibly perpetual peace.

Here are the keys to ensure that you are walking in peace:

- If you are struggling to find peace, you are not alone. Consider the following scriptural advice to help you find or regain that missing peace.

- **Change your focus** - The Bible instructs us to fix "our eyes on Jesus, who leads us and makes our faith complete" (*Hebrews 12:2*). As we change our focus off our problems and onto the Lord, His peace will fill our lives.

- **Change your circumstances** - Sometimes it is necessary to take a break from the things that trouble us even for brief periods of time. Even great men and women of God have at times experienced times of devastating discouragement (*1 Kings 19:3-5; 2 Corinthians 4:7-10*).

  Try altering your physical setting for a short time. Also, take a close look at your lifestyle. You may be lacking peace simply because you are not following God's pattern for rest.

- **Change your attitude** - Are you facing a difficult situation? The Bible says, "Whatever happens, keep thanking God because of Jesus Christ.

  This is what God wants you to do" (*1 Thessalonians 5:18*). Begin to thank God right now and soon you will experience His peace in the midst of the storm.

Jesus wants to give us peace in every storm. In order to have this peace, we must truly understand the gift of peace and have a relationship with the Prince of Peace.

If you do not have a relationship with peace, you will have a relationship with the storms of life. Storms will come, but they don't have to overcome you. Jesus said, "Peace, be still" because He would not allow peace to leave them. Once we know the power of peace, no matter what storm or situation satan tries to bring into your life he cannot rob you of your peace and the storm will not affect you.

The Bible began with peace in the Garden of Eden and closes with peace in eternity. Jesus becomes the peace of all who place their faith in Him. Peace can now reign in the hearts of all those who are His heirs. The peace of Christ is also an unending source of strength in the midst of difficulties.

The work of God begins with peace. Peace is the internal serenity that only God can give. Peace is love in repose, with no borrowing of tomorrow's troubles today.

Troubles are not absent. Rather, God is present! When the Holy Spirit is not grieved, the dove of peace is able to alight on the heart. Has peace become more and more a way of life for you this year?

The peace of Christ is a great resource in helping us to know the will of God. *Colossians 3:15* says, "Let the peace of Christ rule in your hearts, to which indeed you were called in one body; and be thankful."

Paul is urging the Colossians to so depend on the peace of Christ that it becomes an umpire in the decisions they have to make in life. Do you have a problem or a decision to make?

Summary

Let the peace of Christ make that decision for you.

If you have examined a planned action in the light of God's Word and His Word does not forbid you from going ahead with it, do it and retain the peace of Christ in your heart. Then do it with the confidence it is God's will. if you find you do not have a sense of peace and God's blessing about it, do not do it. Do not try to rationalize about your decision; you may find it makes good sense from the rational point of view. Will it rob your soul of rest and peace? Do you have a sense of confidence that God is in this?

If you do not have peace, it is probably the wrong thing to do. Let Christ's peace be the umpire that makes the calls. That is how we are to govern our behavior. If you have a personal relationship with Christ, He is your peace and has promised never to leave nor forsake you. If you bring everything to Him in prayer with thanksgiving, His peace will surround and protect you through every situation *(Philippians 4:6-7)*. If you'll simply look to Him, read His Word, and watch Him work in your life, your heart will be calm — even when your circumstances are anything but.

Chapter 14
How to Enter the Kingdom of God

Introduction

Mankind is a sinful creature; therefore, no man is born without sin. Yet, God proved to us and showed us just how much he loves us. In spite of our sins, he gave his only son in order for us to have eternal life. The purpose of this chapter is to explain the importance of being born again. You will learn that being born again is the only way to enter into the Kingdom of God.

God wants us to have a personal relationship with Him. Although, sin separates us from the relationship that God desires of us, we still have a choice to develop a personal relationship with God by receiving Jesus Christ as our Savior and Lord. We must also repent and ask God to forgive us for our sins.

Upon reading this chapter, you will also learn the importance of water baptism as well as why we should fellowship in a church. I will explain the initial step that must be taken in order to become a citizen in the Kingdom of God.

In order to get the keys to the Kingdom of Heaven, one must be born again and on the following pages the purpose and plan of God will be revealed on how to be born again.

1. **God loves you and you were create you to know Him personally.**

God's Love - "God so loved the world that He gave His only begotten Son, that whoever believes in Him should not perish, but have eternal life" *(John 3:16)*.

God's Plan – "Now this is eternal life: that they may know you, the only true God, and Jesus Christ, whom you have sent" *(John 17:3 NIV)*. What prevents us from knowing God personally?

2. **Man is sinful and separated from God so we cannot know Him personally or experience His love.**

Man is Sinful - "All have sinned and fall short of the glory of God." Man was created to have fellowship with God but because of his own stubborn self-will, he chose to go his own independent way and fellowship with God was broken.

This self-will, characterized by an attitude of active rebellion or passive indifference, is evidence of what the Bible calls sin *(Romans 3:23)*.

Mankind is Separated - "The wages of sin is death" [spiritual separation from God] *(Romans 6:23)*. "...(Those) who do not know God and do not obey the gospel of our Lord Jesus will be punished with everlasting destruction and shut out from the presence of the Lord..." *(2 Thessalonians 1:8-9)*.

3. Jesus Christ is God's only provision for man's sin. Through Him alone we can know God personally and experience God's love.

He Died in Our Place - "God demonstrates His own love toward us, in that while we were yet sinners, Christ died for us" *(Romans 5:8)*.

He Rose From the Dead - "Christ died for our sins... He was buried... He was raised on the third day according to the Scriptures... He appeared to Peter, then to the twelve. After that He appeared to more than five hundred..." *(1 Corinthians 15:1-6)*.

He is the Only Way to God - Jesus said to him, "I am the way, and the truth, and the life; no one comes to the Father, but through me" *(John 14:6)*. It is not enough just to know these truths.

4. We must individually receive Jesus Christ as Savior and Lord. Then we can know God personally and experience His love.

We Must Receive Christ - "As many as received Him, to them He gave the right to become children of God, even to those who believe in His name." *(John 1:12)*

We Receive Christ Through Faith - "By grace you have been saved through faith; and that not of yourselves, it is the gift of God; not as a result of works that no one should boast" *(Ephesians 2:6-9)*. When we receive Christ, we experience a new birth (see *John 3:3-8*).

We Receive Christ by Personal Invitation
Christ speaks "Behold, I stand at the door and knock; if any one hears my voice and opens the door, I will come in to him." *(Revelation 3:20)*

Receiving Christ involves turning to God from self (repentance) and trusting Christ to come into our lives to forgive us of our sins and to make us what He wants us to be. Just to agree intellectually that Jesus Christ is the Son of God and that He died on the cross for our sins is not enough. Nor is it enough to have an emotional experience. We receive Jesus Christ by faith as an act of our will.

You can receive Christ right now by faith through prayer (talking with God). God knows your heart and is not as concerned with your words as He is with the attitude of your heart.

The following is a suggested prayer:

> Lord Jesus, I want to know you personally. Thank you for dying on the cross for my sins. I open the door of my life and receive you as my Savior and Lord. Thank you for forgiving me of my sins and giving me eternal life. Take control of my life. Make me the kind of person you would have me to be.

If you pray this prayer right now, Christ will come into your life as He promised.

How to Know That Christ Is in Your Life

Did you receive Christ into your life? According to His promise in *Revelation 3:20*, where is Christ right now in relation to you? Christ said that He would come into your life and be your friend so you can know Him personally. Would He mislead you? On what authority do you know that God has answered your prayer (the trustworthiness of God himself and His Word)?

The Bible Promises Eternal Life to All Who Receive Christ The witness is that God has given us eternal life, and this life is in His Son. He who has the Son has the life; he who does not have the Son of God does not have the life. These things I have written to you who believe in the name of the Son of God, in order that you may know that you have eternal life." *(1 John 5:11-13)*

Thank God often that Christ is in your life and that He will never leave you *(Hebrews 13:5)*. You can know on the basis of His promise that Christ lives in you and that you have eternal life from the very moment you invite Him in. He will not deceive you. Here is an important reminder — do not depend on feelings.

The promise of God's Word is the Bible--not our feelings are our authority. The Christian lives by faith (trust) in the trustworthiness of God Himself and His Word.

The moment you receive Christ by faith, as an act of your will, many things happened including the following:

1) Christ came into your life *(Revelation 3:20 and Colossians 1:27)*.
2) Your sins were forgiven *(Colossians 1:27)*.
3) You became a child of God *(John 1:12)*.
4) You received eternal life *(John 5:24)*.
5) You began the great adventure for which God created you *(John 10:10; 2 Corinthians 5:17; First Thessalonians 5:18)*.

Can you think of anything more wonderful that could happen to you than entering into a personal relationship with Jesus Christ? Would you like to thank God in prayer right now for what He has done for you? By thanking God, you demonstrate your faith.

Suggestions for Christian Growth

Spiritual growth results from trusting Jesus Christ. "The righteous man shall live by faith" *(Galatians 3:11)*. A life of faith will enable you to trust God increasingly with every detail of your life, and to practice the following:

1. Go to God in prayer daily *(John 15:7)*.
2. Read God's Word daily *(Acts 17:11)* - begin with the Gospel of John.
3. Obey God moment by moment *(John 14:21)*.
4. Witness for Christ by your life and words *(Matthew 4:19; John 15:8)*.
5. Trust God for every detail of your life *(1 Peter 5:7)*.
6. Holy Spirit - Allow Him to control and empower your daily life - witness *(Galatians 5:16-17; Acts 1:8)*.

The Importance of Water Baptism

The view of most evangelical Christian scholars is that salvation is by grace through faith alone. This is especially indicated by **Ephesians 2:8-9, *John 3:16*, and *1 John 5:1***. It is important to understand that baptism is a result of salvation not a cause.

The professing believer should be totally immersed under water. The procedure of immersion is scriptural. The example that we are to follow is found in **Matthew 3:15-17**.

When we do, we find that there is absolutely nothing we can do as humans to earn salvation. **Romans 6:23** tells us that salvation is a "free gift."

We come to Christ through grace by faith (***Ephesians 2:8-9***) and our public baptism brings glory and honor to God. Baptism is an act of obedience and identifying with the death, burial, and resurrection of our Lord and Savior Jesus Christ.

The motivation to pursue baptism should originate from a desire to show to the world an outward demonstration of the person's decision as well as the inward work the Holy Spirit has already begun in us.

An unsaved person would not likely want to be baptized because he would not have the Holy Spirit indwelling him to prompt his desire to follow Christ in obedience (unless a sect or cult group has erroneously taught him or her otherwise).

The fact that one even wants to be baptized (being assured that only faith alone in Jesus Christ saves) is evidence that the Holy Spirit already indwells that person, a result of being born of the Spirit by faith alone.

In the book of Acts, baptism is typically the outward response to coming to faith. It was seen as part of a process, which includes:

1. Hearing (or reading about) the gospel of the Kingdom of God.
2. Being convicted and led by the Holy Spirit to confess one's sins.
3. Coming to faith in Jesus Christ as Savior.
4. Beginning the process of growth (which includes repenting from known sin).
5. Joining a group of believers in a local church fellowship.
6. Being baptized, the last two parts are where there are many different opinions among believers and churches.

You must become a citizen of the Kingdom of God and this is done through receiving the Lord Jesus Christ as your own personal Lord and Savior, by doing this you become born again and a citizen of the Kingdom of God.

Fellowship in a Good Church

<u>Where</u> God's Word admonishes us not to forsake "the assembling of ourselves together..." *(Hebrews 10:25)*. Several logs burn brightly together, but put one aside on the cold hearth and the fire goes out.

So it is with your relationship with other Christians. If you do not belong to a church, do not wait to be invited. Take the initiative. Call the pastor of a nearby church where Christ is honored and His Word is preached. Start this week, and make plans to attend regularly.

Through receiving the Lord Jesus Christ as your own personal Lord and Savior and by doing this you become born again and a citizen of the Kingdom of God.

Summary

We as humans entered into the world as sinners. Glory be to God we can all be delivered from our sin right here on earth. We must be born again and have a personal relationship with God. The only way that is done is to receive Christ into our heart. We receive Christ through faith and through prayer. Faith believes and prayer is talking to God with a sincere heart.

You can pray this prayer with a sincere heart and Christ will come into your life. Lord Jesus, I want to know you personally. Thank you for dying on the cross for my sins. I open the door of my life and I receive you as my own personal Savior and Lord.

Thank you for forgiving me of my sins and giving me eternal life. Take control of my life. Make me the kind of person you want me to be. Jesus will never leave you alone and heaven has become your new home!

The Bible has four spiritual laws that govern our relationship with God just like there are physical laws that govern the universe.

The spiritual laws are:

1. God loves you and offers a wonderful plan for your life *(John 3:16, John 10:10).*
2. Man is sinful and separated from God. Therefore, he cannot know and experience God's love and plan for his life *(Romans 3:23, Romans 6:23).*
3. Jesus Christ is God's only provision for man's sin. Through Him you can know and experience God's love and plan for your life *(Romans 5:8, 1 Corinthians 15:3-6, John 14:6).*
4. We must individually receive Jesus Christ as Savior and Lord; then we can know and experience God's love and plan for our lives *(John 1:12, Ephesians 2:8-9, John 3:1-8, Revelation 3:20).*

Also, remember the suggested steps for Christian growth. It is not an option but an action that must be taken in order to mature in the things of God. We are born as babies in Christ. We must continue to grow spiritually as we do the natural according to the scriptures, which are not a suggestion but a command. Please note the difference between a suggestion and a command. With a suggestion, you have a choice, but with a command, it is an order with no options.

Decision Page

To receive Jesus Christ as your own personal Lord and Savior

The Bible says in *1 John 5:4*, "For whosoever is born of God overcometh the world: and this is the victory that overcometh the world, even our faith. Who is he that overcometh the world, but he that believeth that Jesus is the Son of God"

If yes, on the next few pages there is a list of scriptures to help you to **establish** a relationship with the God and become a citizen of the Kingdom through receiving His only begotten Son Jesus who is the Christ.

As I have shared with you about the subject "The Working of Faith", the only way that you can experience and walk in blessing of God is by receiving the Lord Jesus Christ as your own personal Lord and Savior.

Jesus said "except you are born again yea shall not see the Kingdom of God" according to **John 3:3**.

If you desire to experience "The Victory that overcometh the world" that were covered in this booklet and in the Holy Bible, you must be born-again in order to qualify to enjoy the victory that overcometh the world. According to **1 John 5:4, 5;**

Are you born again?

Listed are some scripture references that you can check out in the Bible to verify what we are saying. There is a short prayer that you can pray to receive the Lord Jesus Christ as your own personal Lord and Savior, and when you do that, you will be born into the Kingdom of God.

Are you born again? Have you ever received Jesus as your Lord and Savior? If the answer to this question is no, read these scriptures and pray this prayer, agreeing with it and believing it from your heart

John 3:16 "For God so loved the world, that he gave his only begotten Son, that whosoever believeth in him should not perish, but have everlasting life"

Romans 10:9-10, 13 "That if thou shalt confess with thy mouth the Lord Jesus, and shalt believe in thine heart that God hath raised him from the dead, thou shalt be saved.

For with the heart man believeth unto righteousness; and with the mouth **Confession** is made unto salvation. For whosoever shall call upon the name of the Lord shall be saved.

John 14:6 " Jesus said unto him, I am the way, the truth and the life: no man cometh unto the Father, but by me."

PRAY THIS PRAYER

Dear God in Heaven, I come to you believing that Jesus Christ died on the cross for man's sins. I open my heart and invite Jesus to come in to be my personal Lord and Savior. Jesus, forgive me for all my sins and cleanse me from all unrighteousness. Teach me God's Word, and fill me with the power of the Holy Spirit. Give me knowledge and wisdom, and show me how to live a victorious life. I thank You, Jesus, because I am born again and saved through your shed blood on the cross at Calvary. I am on my way to heaven in the name of Jesus.

Signed _____ Date _____

Endnotes

Bible, King James Vision (1997) containing the Old Testament and New Testament Authorized King James Version Red-Letter, Illinois: Tyndale House Publication

Rediscovering the Kingdom by Dr. Myles Munroe

Bishop Earthquake Kelley, Bound to Lose Destined to Win (CopperScroll Publishers, LLC, 2007)

Freddy Vest "A Rodeo Cowboy's Fight to Survive" http://www.cbn.com/700club/features/amazing/AR99_Freddy_Vest.aspx

Jesse Duplantis, Heaven- Close Encounters of the God Kind (Tulsa, OK: Harrison House, 1996)

Spirit Jurisdiction by Marcus Bishop, (Marcus Bishop Ministries, Panama City Beach, Florida 1996)

About the Author

Pastor\Author James L. Monteria is a born-again ordained Minister of the Gospel. He is a graduate of Rhema Bible Training Center of Broken Arrow, a suburb of Tulsa, Oklahoma, where he earned a Diploma in Ministerial Training. Pastor Monteria received his Bachelor of Science degree in Business Administration from Saint Paul's College in Lawrenceville, VA. He received a Master of Instructional Education degree from Central Michigan University, Mount Pleasant, Michigan. Pastor Monteria has ministered the Word of God through church services, Bible studies, prison ministries, seminars, and book, CD, and DVD distributions.

Pastor Monteria believes that the Bible is the Word of God, and he is an anointed Pastor and Teacher of the Word of God. His ministries are a combination of anointed preaching and teaching the Word of God and flowing in the gifts of the Holy Spirit as the lead.

Pastor\Author J. L. Monteria
Speaking Engagements ~Workshops ~ Conferences
Mailing Address - P. O. Box 932, Chesterfield, VA, 23832
Website - **www.clmministries.org**
Email - **comeandlearnofme@gmail.com**

www.ingramcontent.com/pod-product-compliance
Lightning Source LLC
Chambersburg PA
CBHW070757100426
42742CB00012B/2165